A PERSONAL GOD:

You're Not Alone

A
PERSONAL
GOD:

You're Not Alone

BARRY KOLANOWSKI

XULON PRESS

Xulon Press
2301 Lucien Way #415
Maitland, FL 32751
407.339.4217
www.xulonpress.com

Paperback ISBN-13: 978-1-66284-419-5
Ebook ISBN-13: 978-1-66284-420-1

Dedication

It is an honor to dedicate this book to the most personable person I have ever met, my Mother-in-Law, Marlis Hutchinson. There has never been a time that she didn't make me feel special and welcome. Her interest in others goes without equal.

That interest goes beyond listening or questions. She is an avid sew-er, a rare commodity for today, and she uses her current project is to use her sewing machine almost daily to supply hurting and challenged individuals with hats or cloth handbags that can be connected to a wheelchair or walker.

She is in her 90's yet she has a stream of energy to sew her bags, post-surgical pillows and even comforting cloth dolls. And always finds time to attend her activities as a volunteer or participant.

She amazes me with her selfless attitude and generous heart. She finds time to attend church during the week and on Sundays with a focus on a very personal God who notices her every stitch.

Thank you, mom, for being such loving example.

Table of Content

About the Author

BARRY KOLANOWSKI HAS spent over twenty years as a minister studying the Bible. He acted as chaplain for the Morris, Illinois Police Department where he faced some of the most horrific life situations. Then he spent nearly a decade with the American Cancer Society, where he rose to the position of Regional Director over their local unit. Finally, he was the CEO for the Senior Services of Will County for six years.

The one thing he found in common in all the various occupations was that when people were facing a difficulty, they felt like God didn't care or had no interest in them unless they were big contributors. There was an overall feeling that God was distant. But that is far from the fact. He is not only right there with you, but He also hurts when you hurt. This entire book was written to help set the record straight.

Since he left Senior Services, he is offering his experiences with those who will listen. Either by limited personal talks or through his books of various topics. If you are interested in having his unique presentation live, please feel free to contact him at 630.392.1953 or by email at revbarry1234@gmail.com.

He ran his own consulting business and saved Senior Services from bankruptcy causing an auditor to proclaim, "this is a one million dollar turn around on one year, unheard of in nonprofit industry." He offers several publications. A three-training set, It's All About the Smile (customer service)," "It's All About the Dance (sales)," or "It's All About the Shout (marketing)."

He also has performed as a keynote speaker alongside the topics of his other books: "Pause: Lessons about How To Get What You Want Out of Life," "The Seven Sales Secrets for Non-Salespeople," or finally because of his extensive award winning work with social services he explains the paradigm that he used in working with Senior Services of Will County in his book, "Nonprofit Nonsense: Charities in Crisis."

If you would like to be added to his conference schedule for presentations in your area or would like more information, please let him know.

"Cast all your anxiety on Him because he cares for you." — *I Peter 5:7*

Foreword
By Rev. John Ciesniewski

I LOVE NATURE because I've always believed that it's in nature that I will best encounter God. For example:

- There is a forest preserve not too far from where I live and it's in that forest preserve where you will often find me taking long walks while talking with God and looking for God during his creation.
- If I'm near an ocean, it's likely you'll find me walking along the shoreline in the early morning hours waiting expectantly for God's creation to rise above the horizon and bring warmth to my body.
- I've hiked the Grand Canyon twice and can't wait to plan my next trip because whether I'm at the top looking down and across or at the bottom looking up and over, I am captivated at

God's creation and believe I will encounter him in a deep and personal way.

- And every summer since my middle son who is now 19 was just two, our family would take a bi-annual trip to my in-law's farm in a remote part of Eastern Iowa. At night, my boys and I would lay on the driveway for hours looking up into the night sky and marveling over God's creation and straining to take in the Milky Way.

Again, at least for me, I've always associated nature with God, his presence, and his power. And while that's true sometimes, it's not true all the time because sometimes God makes himself available in the most unexpected and unlikely places – places of loss, fatigue, darkness, illness, and loneliness. In fact, singer and songwriter Danny Gokey conveys this better than most through his song, "More Than You Think I Am."

You always think I'm somewhere on a mountaintop, but never behind bars. You'd be amazed the places that I go to be with you where you are. So, forget what you've heard, what you think that you know. There's a lot about Me that's never been told

I'm more than you dream
More than you understand
Your days and your times
Were destined for our dance.

I catch all your tears
Burn your name on my heart
Be still and trust my plan
I'm more than you think I am

As you'll soon discover, God is indeed more than you might think. He's deeply personal, ever present and meets us in the least likely places – places that my friend Barry Kolanowski has been and is about to take you. I trust you'll find Barry's journey and encounter with God encouraging, hopeful and maybe even an answer to your prayer.

Forward by Pastor and Author John Ciesniewski, author of the book, "Discover Hope" a book about stress and recovery

Jesus Loves Me This I know

Jesus loves me this I know,
for the Bible tells me so.
Little ones to Him belong,
they are weak, but He is strong.

Preface

Meeting A Personal God.

IT IS ALMOST a contradiction of terms. To think that God who is high and lifted up can be personal and individual at the same time is hard to comprehend. But He is. We tend to pick one way of relating to and seeing Him: either through His power, or His love. It may be beyond us, but we live in an age of awakening, faced with so-called truth on all sides. The statements we hear can infuriate us at times and at other times simply confirm what we already believed to be true. A friend of mine and I once heard a motivational speak, and then recessed for a quick lunch in my car. As we sat there munching down our takeout meals, and I commented how much I had enjoyed the speaker. My friend responded with a question that has had me evaluating all of my judgements since then: "Was he that good a presenter, or did he just simply agree with your set of beliefs?"

One of the problems we face as a society today is that what we accept and what we reject might both be true. Fake news has filled our media, and our minds. Since the Watergate days of President Nixon, we have been a generation of conspiracy theorists, and trust in any authority figure has become a luxury. According to one recent poll 49% of Americans link the decline in interpersonal trust to a belief that people are not as reliable as they used to be. So, when relating to God, we create a version of him that fits our perception instead of the facts found in the Bible. As a result, we have as many perceptions of God as we do images of Santa Claus. Each one minimizes Him making Him meek and distant, that He is a weak being who is uninvolved in our lives and tolerates all of our indulgences.

One stunning truth may be in our perception of God because we don't understand God's actions, or what we see as inaction, and we move to make Him so we make Him even more impersonal than ever. This separation means we feel safer and protects our understanding of God. He is so awesome and unknowable, that He is a far off. We push Him away and keep Him at arm's length so we can continue our liberty to do what we want, when we want. The result is that we don't fully experience His love because we don't have intimacy with him. We reduced our image of God to a genie in the bottle responding to our whims.

The truth is the Bible gives us a glimpse of a very personal and emotional God, deeply connected to His us:

> *"For we have not a high priest which cannot be touched with the feeling of our infirmities; but was in all points tempted like as we are, yet without sin." — Hebrews 4:15 KJV*

God is touched by our pain. He knows you and cares about you, but most of all He is touched by your uncertainty in times of a crisis, pain in heart, body, and your anger at those who would want to hurt you. Your pain may have successfully buried the hurt deep in your psyche (or like me in my humor when uncomfortable), but it is still with you, troubling you with self-doubt.

The Dread of isolation at night

Worry always seems to rear its head at night. We can function during the daylight hours in front of our friends or coworkers and in a spiritual sense have covered it with make-up. But it affects our decisions in ways we don't recognize or understand. That pressure of worry in life makes us do things that keep the pressure on and makes us a victim.

In the hours before Jesus' arrest, he was in the Garden of Gethsemane with his closest friends. That evening he had predicted to his disciples his coming death and resurrection in detail. It was clearly on His mind what the hours ahead would mean to Him. He asked his friends to come aside and pray with him during this difficult hour:

> *"Then Jesus went with his disciples to a place called Gethsemane, and he said to them, "Sit here while I go over there and pray." He took Peter and the two sons of Zebedee along with him, and he began to be sorrowful and troubled. Then he said to them, "My soul is overwhelmed with sorrow to the point of death. Stay here and keep watch with me." Going a little farther, he fell with his face to the ground and prayed, "My Father, if it is possible, may this cup be taken from me. Yet not as I will, but as you will." Then he returned to his disciples and found them sleeping. "Couldn't you men keep watch with me for one hour?" he asked Peter." — Matthew 26:36 – 40 NIV*

Jesus was Disappointed

Can you feel the disappointment in the words of Jesus? He was feeling the weight of his last hours, one account found in the Bible even describes Him as sweating blood during this time. He had confided to

His disciples His strength of Spirit, but weakness of flesh and asked for their help. Instead, they slept, and in His moment of vulnerability when he needed his friends most, they disappointed Him. Jesus opened His heart, and was let down.

Today though He is not far off from us. Jesus knows our emotional pain, and cares. God is a very personal God, intimately familiar with heartache. We may have been there disappointed by the actions and responses of friends in the midst of our challenges and pain, just as Jesus was. However, Jesus will never leave us.

In this book we will chronicle examples of God's feelings, and look at his understanding of deep pain. In our times of difficulty, we may think God doesn't know or doesn't care about our pain and even that we are alone. He not only know us, and is aware of our pain, He deeply cares for us, is with us in our sorrow, hurts with us, and gives us strength to overcome

> *"For I know the thoughts that I think toward you, saith the Lord, thoughts of peace, and not of evil, to give you an expected end. Then shall ye call upon me, and ye shall go and pray unto me, and I will hearken unto you. And ye shall seek me, and find me, when ye shall search for me with all your heart." — Jeremiah 29:11-13 KJV*

These words of Jeremiah are an encouragement to us in times of difficulty, but it is also important for us to understand the context in which they were written.

They had no choice

At the time of his writing, ancient Israel had been taken into slavery by the Babylonian armies. They were held for seventy years, and as captives had to do as they were instructed by their masters. This was not the first time Israel had faced adversity, but the experience of it was different. Earlier in history, when Assyria had conquered Israel, the Assyrians remained in Israel and intermarried with them. But when Babylon, conquered Israel, they took the brightest and best-looking Israelites back to their own country in chains to benefit from their talents and skills, leaving only the poor and least talented behind. It is within this context that Jeremiah pens these radical verses of hope.

While in Babylon they had no free-will, but here was a promise of redemption: God had a plan. As difficult as the Israelite's experience was, God was declaring through Jeremiah, "I know it is hard and I feel your pain but some day this will end."

We may not know how the trials will end up, but God does, and He feels it with us. He is not as far off as we may feel or think, but He is alongside us, as the familiar poem below reads:

"Footprints in the Sand"

"One night I dreamed a dream.
As I was walking along the beach with my Lord.
Across the dark sky flashed scenes from my life.
For each scene, I noticed two sets of footprints in the sand,
One belonging to me and one to my Lord.

After the last scene of my life flashed before me,
I looked back at the footprints in the sand.
I noticed that at many times along the path of my life,
especially at the very lowest and saddest times,
there was only one set of footprints.

This really troubled me, so I asked the Lord about it. "Lord, you said once I decided to follow you, 'You'd walk with me all the way. But I noticed that during the saddest and most troublesome times of my life, there was only one set of footprints. I don't understand why, when I needed You the most, You would leave me.' He whispered, "My precious child, I love you and will never leave you, Never, ever, during your trials and testing. When you saw only one set of footprints, It was then that I carried you."

— Author Mary Stevenson

God carries you

The authorship has long been debated, but the principles have not. He is right with you. A firefighter carries the gold standard of moving someone out of harm's way. Made famous by the occupation, this type of carry should only be conducted by a very strong rescuer. A firefighter of over twenty years commented on the best way to carry someone to safety, saying,

"The relocating of people away from risky or deadly incidents is an essential component of my job. Among the seemingly endless tactics, a firefighter is taught from day one, (and) the ability to remove someone from harm is near the top of the list. Life safety is the top priority."

Firefighters follow their training when in crisis, which means he has to weigh their every action with the potential harm or injury to themselves and their at-risk person. God has no such concern. Your weight, the level of His strength, or your state of consciousness is no worry to him as he carries you.

Consider the often quoted psalm:

> "He makes me lie down in green pastures, he leads me beside quiet waters, he refreshes my soul. He guides me along the right paths for his name's sake. Even though I walk through the darkest valley, I will fear

no evil, for you are with me;" — Psalm
23:2-4 *NIV*

He is with us even during bad times

Throughout scripture we see this promise of God's presence in our lives proclaimed. God is not far off. In the book of Deuteronomy, Moses reminds us:

> *"and in the wilderness. There you saw how the Lord your God carried you, as a father carries his son, all the way you went until you reached this place." — Deuteronomy 1:31 NIV*

Here God tells us that we aren't just cared for but carried like a father carries his son, a picture full of tenderness. We can cling to this truth and the reality of God's love for us during our pain. In the book of Romans, Paul encourages us that what we may be suffering through today, but it will turn out better than we can imagine. In God's kindness, he will take our suffering and use it for good. Paul writes:

> *"And we know that in all things God works for the good of those who love him, who have been called according to his purpose."* — Romans 8:28 KJV

We don't have to understand how God will work things for our good, we just must trust that he will. He is waiting for us to turn to him, he will walk through the journey with us.

A few months ago I had a stroke. When it happened I soon found myself lying in a hospital bed, shocked at what just occurred. One minute I was fine, I even walked into the emergency department and laid down on the bed myself, not knowing or expecting it to be the last time I would walk on my own power for four weeks.

I felt alone. I am a man of faith, but I felt short-changed by God. I had known uncertainties in life before, but this was different, and I wasn't a resilient young man any longer. The stroke left me paralyzed on one side, and my speech was slurred. I feared for my job, what company concerned with looks, mobility, or stamina would hire me? My wife Julie was very supportive, but I felt alone and wanted to be strong for her.

In the emergency room, when the doctor first confirmed that I was having a stroke, he explained that due to the position of the clot, it meant any intervention was impossible. They would have to let the stroke take its course, and he went on to say it would get worse before it got better. They moved me to a place of isolation, pulled the tented curtain closed, and left me alone. No wonder they expressed a fear of depression, I felt completely helpless. Those words, the prognosis, and lack of treatment removed any positive thinking on my part and I expected to die.

I felt discarded

The word to describe how I felt in that moment was, discarded. When my doctor came to check-in and my daughter asked a simple question, the physician turned away from me, pretended I wasn't in the room, and answered, "what do you expect he is 68?" It felt as though I was already gone. Trying to get past the negativity surrounding me it all felt like I was swimming upstream. I thought to myself is this really how it ends? Will I really die?

> *"But who are you, a human being, to talk back to God? "Shall what is formed say to the one who formed it, 'Why did you make me like this?'" Does not the potter have the right to make out of the same lump of clay some pottery for special purposes and some for common use?" — Romans 9:20-21 NIV*

On the third day in my hospital bed, I was watching a religious program and I saw a television minister say that God had great plans for me, even if I didn't see them now. Those words gave me hope during my hopelessness. I felt grateful for God's presence with me, I felt empowered that somehow God had selected me to have a stroke knowing I could handle it, I could overcome it, and I could somehow be used to inspire others with the good news that Jesus loves me.

I didn't know the challenges still waiting ahead, but suddenly my attitude changed toward the positive. I was in the valley of death, and now I felt I was chosen for a purpose. I must get well. I have never felt closer to the Lord. He is a very personal God who comes to us in times of trouble. Though I am not healed, I knew he was with me.

My challenges did not end with a gaining back of my physical health. My workplace had communicated with me, they sent me flowers, a card, and even visited me with the assurance that my work continued and was waiting for me. Within four weeks I was given a Return-to-Work form from my doctor, but my employer encouraged me to stay home and take my time. I believed them and concentrated on improving my speech and mobility. Then came the call to attend a meeting. At the meeting I was told I was being "retired." I was shocked by the news, then hurt, as my six years of tenure suddenly meant little. Again, I felt discarded, and what I saw as simply a delay in returning, they saw as terminal.

It took me some time to sort out my feelings, then a passage from Genesis gave me some comfort. It was near the end of the story of Joseph. His brothers at one point in their lives had conspired against him. Years later, Joseph helped his brothers escape a dangerous famine, but as the brothers feared for their lives because of their father's pending death, the brothers remembered their earlier betrayal of Joseph when their jealousy led them to act unkindly toward him. Now, in his position of power, he had the power to act out with revenge. Instead, Joseph spoke these words:

> *"But as for you, ye thought evil against me;*
> *but God meant it unto good, to bring to pass,*
> *as it is this day, to save many people alive."*
> — Genesis 50:20 KJV

A more promising future

I opened this preface with Anna Warner's simple poem, Jesus Loves Me. It has become the best-loved Christian hymn ever composed, and has been translated into more languages than any other hymn. After 160 years, it remains the number one children's spiritual song around the world, and the simplicity of its message still speaks to millions of adults worldwide.

As barriers come there is none created by man that is as impressive as the Great Wall of China. It is a series of fortifications that were built across the historical northern borders of ancient Chinese states and gave Imperial China great protection against various nomadic groups around 7 BC. But basically, and ideally, it was to keep the Chinese people separate from the rest of the world. The frontier walls were built by different dynasties and have multiple courses. Collectively, they stretch across the landscape for about 13,171 miles and can be seen from space. The irony of the walls to keep the kingdom safe is well known. As much as the walls were strong it became the security at the gates that were the weak points. It allowed potential invaders a point of entry and all it took was a simple bribe to let them in.

What we let in the various gates of our lives determine how secure we really are. Do we spend an enormous amount of time building up our walls thinking we are safe but ignore the gates? And so, it is with humanity. God stands in the open calling to us, the same call He does today. Will you respond or will you hide?

Introduction

A minister who wanted to watch what he considered to be an important clash between two of his favorite sports teams was clearly frustrated. He knew that his schedule didn't allow him to view the game, and with remorse he realized he couldn't be in two places at once. His wife noticed his down spirit and inquired the reason, and he explained his problem in detail. His wife had a simple solution and suggested he record the event and watch it later.

He was surprised at how easily he could solve his trouble, and embraced her plan, making sure he would not do anything to learn the outcome of the game until he viewed his recording. The minister went on with his scheduled commitments as planned. At one of his appointments, he ran into someone from church who, trying to convey excitement and celebrate with a friend, shouted out, "Hey what a game they won!" At first, the minister was happy to learn his team had won, but then it sank in that he hadn't had a chance to see the game play out himself. He handled his responsibilities and later, with reluctance because he already knew the outcome, he turned on the television and started to watch his recording of the game.

Then came a change of attitude. He went from disappointment to delight. All because he knew the ultimate outcome of the game in advance. Every play of the game was affected by his prior knowledge, and it completely changed his perspective of the game. Every fumble, every interception, didn't matter, they had won! As bad as the game may have seemed at times, he knew it did not change the final score. In the end his team would still win. His disappointment to have learned the game's results in advance was quickly replaced with joy, and even times of laughter as he watched the team make a blunder here and there.

Toward the end of the recording, the minister began thinking about his own life. He considered how on a dark Friday afternoon Jesus's death had to have been seen as terrible, and it was. For those present, it must have been the worst of days. But the minister knew that in three days Jesus would rise from the dead and the game would be over. If his disciples had only realized that Jesus would win in the end, it would have changed their viewpoint on everything.

They would have been filled with anticipation on the Saturday of that weekend. The disciples did share the

Sabbath together, depressed, but then Sunday dawned, when they the news from the women, they would have been like children on Christmas morning, brimming with excitement to see their presents under the tree. They would run to be the first at the tomb to welcome Jesus' back. Instead, because they did not know the outcome, they were in hiding. Scared, confused, and wondering about their future.

This book is for us. It is to remind us that in the end, we win. Every play has been completed, every battle has been fought, and every fumble has already happened. The outcome is we win. Understanding this importance of this perspective is incredible. Consider the challenges of our own life they are only temporary, the final play has not been called. In the end what was faced in this life will be erased.

We win

It was illustrated in the story of Lazarus being raised from the dead as found in the Bible in the book of Luke 11. When Jesus received word, that Lazarus was sick and near death, the disciple's thought Jesus would drop everything and hurry to Lazarus' side. But instead he continued speaking and caring for the needy, for a full four days, By the time they arrived at the home of Lazarus not only he had died but the Bible tells us graphically, he smelled. The reason for the delay of Jesus seemed hard to understand to Lazarus' sister Martha.

When Jesus first arrived at the village, she met Him outside of town and shouted at Jesus because He had intentionally delayed His return. But Jesus knew how the game would end. In fact, He timed His returned to provide maximum impact right when the body was decaying, and no one could accuse Him of a parlor trick or that Lazarus had not really died, only fainted.

No matter how dark things seem to be for us right now, the final score is tabulated. Take heart knowing that in the end we will be counted among the victors when we trust in Jesus. We win. And I say that while I limp, with a lazy left hand and experience the ravages of a stroke. Someday, the effects of my stroke will be over, and I win.

Please enjoy the new perspective this book provides. God cares about us and is aware of our circumstances. We are not alone. Every chapter in this book is a proclamation that we win!

Out for a Stroll

"Lift up your eyes and look to the heavens: Who created all these? He who brings out the starry host one by one and calls forth each of them by name. Because of his great power and mighty strength, not one of them is missing." — Isaiah 40:26 NIV

DOCTORS HAVE TOLD us repeatedly of the value to bodily and mental well-being, that a simple daily walk can have an amazing impact on our overall health. In response, we grumble and drag ourselves to the gym to grind out the miles, weary of boredom and eyeing the progress of those around us, wondering what the fuss is all about. There are over 100 million people, almost half of America, that take this daily charge seriously, and by faith continue taking steps each day, trusting that their efforts will add up to the promised benefits.

We understand now through the lenses of research and statistics that the health and mental benefits of walking are significant. But walking can also be a time of great connection, when done with others. Often overlooked as insignificant in the story found in the Bible and the book of Genesis, we see God walking in the Garden of Eden as a picture of his love and residence among his creation, marking the kind of relationship he had at one time with man.

> *"And they heard the <u>voice</u> of the Lord God <u>walking</u> in the garden in the cool of the day..."* — Genesis 3:8 NIV

It Was Heaven On Earth

It is hard to picture a more idyllic scene than this. Creation was complete the stars were fixed in their place, the earth's vegetation untampered with, and animals lived in peace, sleeping side-by-side. God had punctuated each day of creation with the words, "it is good," declaring the work to be complete, and glorious. At that time, God called out plainly to man. There was no separation between them, Adam and Eve had full access to the Lord. When He spoke and they heard the loving voice of their Creator.

But things were about to turn. Man's greediness brought an abrupt end to the freedom of communing with God in the Garden. The serpent wanted to tarnish this relationship by intentionally misstating God's command to Eve. He was purposely casting doubt in the minds of Adam and Eve and causing them to question God's guidance. Creating the first conspiracy theory.

Adam and Eve wanted more than what God had provided and chose to believe He was holding something back from them. They wanted to experience what he had forbidden, and ultimately chose to believe the lies of the serpent, following their own desires rather than trust in God's care for them. Their choice brought separation from God to all generations, like a virus.

It is hard to imagine that just one person could be responsible for such an impact on humanity, but in the days of Covid-19 it gave us some insight into how the effects of original sin can spread from one person throughout creation. In a recent article in the journal, Science, it identifies a single vendor from the Huanan Seafood Wholesale Market in Wuhan, China as the first person to contract the Covid-19 virus. From there it spread and became a world-wide pandemic that the global community continues to grapple with. The effects of sin spread in a similar manner. Adam and Eve's decision to rebel against God introduced sin to the human experience, and would begin to ravage the lives of all people. Even science researchers recently acknowledge that the omicron variant of the covid-19 virus may well infect everyone with varying degrees of intensity.

God wanted to be closer

In Genesis, we clearly see the level of intimacy God had established and intended to have with His creation. He strolled in the Garden, he spoke to Adam and Eve with no intermediary, he dwelled with them and was fully present. No separation or barrier existed after creation, until the disobedience of man. It was our choice to put God at a distance, we caused it, not God.

God and man would no longer walk in the garden together. The separation began, and made direct contact with Him impossible. But God found another way to speak to His creation. We see these ways woven throughout the Bible. He used a burning bush to talk to Moses, then he selected Prophets to act as His spokesmen, and there was a quiet whisper with which He comforted Elijah. The finger of God at Mt. Sinai provided us with the Ten Commandments, even the donkey of Balaam was given the ability to speak a warning. But never did he speak like He did at the beginning in the Garden. Finally, He gave us The Bible and it became God's revelation to us. It was a love letter leading us to Him. It is God-breathed and gives us access to learn about Him and his character whenever we desire, it allows us to hear from him. No app or charging required.

Through the Bible, and through prayer, you can speak to Him, and He to you without limitation no matter where you are. In a jail cell, in church, the master bedroom or even on a hospital bed. When you wake up in the middle of the night all alone, or when you're with a group of people. This book is a reminder of God's love to us.

But God's plan has always been our redemption, and the restoration of our relationship to Him. He accomplished this through Jesus, who took on human form and lived among us. Not since the Garden of Eden had God walked among and spoken directly to us. In the Garden of Eden God foretold the coming of redemption. He promised Eve that her offspring would one day, bruise the head of the serpent and restore that personal relationship God once had with people. In that way he could once again convey His heart directly.

When I was a kid a popular game of the time was telephone. We would gather with friends and form two lines, then a phrase was whispered to the first person of each line, not to be overheard. At the signal of go, the first person would turn and tell the second person what they thought they heard. The second person then whispered to the third, and so on down the line. The last person did their very best to share the phrase as they heard it, and in the end the statement was always hilarious. No matter how serious the phrase, and how hard we tried to get it right, we all ended up laughing at the mistakes made along the way.

God doesn't want His message misunderstood. He wants to share His message clearly with His people. We went from a walk in the Garden, to Jesus walking on the streets of Jerusalem. God was half-way back to the original relationship that put Him in touch with mankind. Then to increase His Presence He chose twelve disciples, spending time with the twelve then a group of seventy, and at the last a group of over 500, teaching them His ways. Jesus sent them out to literally touch more people. Finally, He sent the Holy Spirit down to make possible that every Christ follower could enjoy some level of His presence.

He cares. He is still reaching out. When we are reading the Bible, and we feel drawn to Him, know that is the Holy Spirit speaking to us through the printed page. He wasn't walking in the Garden that day to catch Adam in the act. He wasn't working out or exercising for His physical and mental health. He was looking forward to a conversation with His favorite creation.

He wants to hear about our wins and losses, He is listening when we have a broken heart or when we are joyfully happy. He wants to share our life experience with us. Most of all, he wants to put his arms around us and comfort us. He said these words in John 14, even though he knew He was about to be crucified:

> *"Do not let your hearts be troubled. You
> believe in God believe also in me."* —
> John 14:1 NIV

Can you walk away from love?

Listen to the heart cry of God reaching out to us.
How can we walk away from love? That was what I
thought the first time I was told Jesus loved me. I was
raised in a largely non-attending Catholic home. At age
eighteen and I was so sure of myself. I had a job and a car.
The two things I thought I needed most in high school.
There was a philosophy teacher at my high school that I
admired and so I embraced all his faiths and belief sys-
tems. One night I was out with a friend and we went
to a movie together with the promise I would meet his
minister friend. We went to a local restaurant where I
was introduced to a youth minister. He went right for
my spiritual jugular vein. He spoke about the love God
had for me and asked me my reaction.

My first thought was to engage him in a philosophical debate about the religions of the world and I told
him so. But he led off the discussion with love, God's
love for me. Not judgement or condemnation, not religious fervor. Faced with only Jesus' radical love for me,
I was tongue tied. The debate was over and there in a
restaurant amidst all the noise, I bowed my head and

prayed asking God to forgive my indifference and party lifestyle becoming a Christ follower.

If you would have asked me as an 18-year-old what I was going to do with my life, before that moment I would have spoken to you about my acceptance into the AFROTC program at Southern Illinois University and my hopes of one day flying to space. But my decision that night changed my life's trajectory. I have been walking with God ever since. And God desires to walk with you too, through the difficulties, the upsets, the heartache and grief, and also through the joy.

In What Ways Does God Prove He
Cares About Me?

_____

_____

_____

_____

_____

_____

_____

_____

_____

_____

_____

_____

_____

_____

_____

_____

_____

_____

God Has Plans for You

*"What other nation is so great as to have
their gods near them the way the Lord our
God is near us whenever we pray to him?"*
— Deuteronomy 4:7 NIV

THERE MAY BE a time when God lays something on
your heart for you to do for others. Your first response
to this sense of calling might be fear, and you may find
yourself doubting your abilities to bring what's been laid
on your heart to fruition. This can be discouraging but
recognizing our limitations and needs in this way can
help us rely on the presence and power of God in our
everyday lives. As he provides the strength we need, we
experience him as a personal God, intimately present
and involved in our lives.

God loves to work through is people to touch the
lives of others. By doing so, both groups of people are
impacted. Think about the last time you voluntarily

helped someone. It doesn't have to be a formal volunteer opportunity, but something as simple as helping your grandmother carry in her groceries. You felt good right? Small and random acts of kindness such as this are examples of the ways God can use us to show his love to others. In doing so, our hearts are impacted as well.

A booklet called, *Scouting is for Boys,* dating back to 1908 by co-authors Baden and Powell was assembled for the Boy Scouts organization, and it encourages all people to find time to do a good deed. This might be as simple helping an old woman to cross the street, or to make room on a seat for someone. But it goes on to caution that we accept no reward for the duty. in return. Maybe you have been a recipient of such kindness.

Whether it be small opportunities as mentioned in the comments above, or in larger opportunities where we may question our ability to complete the task, God can use the resources and skills He has placed in our lives for the good of others. Even when we feel we may be lacking, God will provide us with strength as we work to accomplish what he has placed on our hearts.

In the book of Jeremiah, we see that the prophet also questioned his ability to undertake the project God had placed on his heart, and that God helped equip him:

> *"Then the Lord reached out his hand and touched my mouth and said to me, "I have put my words in your mouth. See, today I*

appoint you over nations and kingdoms to uproot and tear down, to destroy and over- throw, to build and to plant." — Jeremiah 1:9-10 NIV

God has plans for you

God's plans for Jeremiah impacted a kingdom. He has plans for your life too. Turn your focus away from your doubt and feelings of inadequacy, and focus instead on your trust and strength in God and the work he wants to do through you. We are meant to serve and care for our enemies as well. The Bible is clear when it says it is easy to help nice people, but there is a special reward in the caring for those with whom you do not get along with easily.

God will make sure you have the means or skills. It may not be easy, and it may require faith on your part, but God will meet you. In Jeremiah, we see the willing- ness of the prophet, and how God equipped him. God "touched him," a very personal act taking a spiritual hot coal from the altar and pressing it against his lips. In doing so, He gave him authority over his world.

Notice the words of the Apostle Paul as he tells us about God's willingness to equip you.

"…to equip his people for works of service, so that the body of Christ may be built up." — Ephesians 4:12 NIV

His appointment was about life, so he could help others. What is important for us to understand is that God's focus is on love, not on judgement. That was a hard concept for me to understand. My perception of God all my life was that I lived precariously under a "Thor-like" hammer which could fall at any time. I believed if there was a God, and He would take delight in punishing me. But once I surrendered to the Son and studied His ways, I found He was a loving savior.

One preacher put it this way, "I pray as though it all depends on God and work as though it all depends on me.". God will equip us, but it will require effort from us as well. We should be ready for anything and that is not limited to spiritual things. There are whole group of people that are prepared if there is an economic or military disaster. They stock up almost to a cult-like level and they're called "preppers."

Are you a prepper?

A person who is defined by Google as a "prepper" is a person who believes a disaster or emergency is likely to occur in the distant future and makes active preparations for it. Typically, they are stockpiling food, ammunition, and other supplies. There's no agreement among preppers about what disaster is most imminent. The point is they are ready. But with no pending zombie apocalypse on the horizon unless there is local disaster it is an expensive exercise.

Again, this points to a relationship. Consider the words of Jesus regarding the lilies of the field. One could be like a "prepper," depending solely on myself or there is faith.

> *"Consider how the wildflowers grow. They do not labor or spin. Yet I tell you, not even Solomon in all his splendor was dressed like one of these. If that is how God clothes the grass of the field, which is here today, and tomorrow is thrown into the fire, how much more will he clothe you—you of little faith!" — Luke 12: 27-28 NIV*

Did you stand in front of the mirror after you dressed to see how you did? Did you check out the military gig lines to make sure they were straight? We put so much attention toward our appearance because it matters to us. But does God put emphasis on clothes? How much will He cloth us? If God cares so much about our clothing which is in fashion, wears out, and is tossed away, how much more does He provide for our food and housing? He cares for us.

You might not feel worthy

We may have many excuses that keep us staying home, instead of finding ways to serve. But when we choose to engage, we connect our lives to others. Doing so can bring us peace and draw us closer to God. May people believe God dwells in the brick and mortar of a church building, but he also dwells in the ways we commune with him and others.

God saw need all around Him.

> *"For I was hungry, and you gave me something to eat, I was thirsty, and you gave me something to drink, I was a stranger and you invited me in, I needed clothes and you clothed me, I was sick, and you looked after me, I was in prison and you came to visit me.' Then the righteous will answer him, 'Lord, when did we see you hungry and feed you, or thirsty and give you something to drink? When did we see you a stranger and invite you in, or needing clothes and clothe you? When did we see you sick or in prison and go to visit you?' The King will reply, 'Truly I tell you, whatever you did for one of the least of these brothers and sisters of mine, you did for me.'"* — Matthew 26:35-40 NIV

Jesus is closest to us when we serve others. If we don't see Him in our life, we may not be fully looking. He is visiting the lost in prison, the sick in hospitals, the homeless in the streets, and the naked in the shelters. We can find him there.

In What Ways Does God Prove He Cares About Me?

_____

_____

_____

_____

_____

_____

_____

_____

_____

_____

_____

_____

_____

_____

_____

_____

When Things Get Tough

> *"Many will be purified, made spotless and refined, but the wicked will continue to be wicked. None of the wicked will understand, but those who are wise will understand."* — Daniel 12:10 NIV

IN THE OLD Testament book of Daniel, we find the well-known story of Shadrach, Meshach, and Abednego: three Hebrew slaves who were cast into a fiery furnace by a furious king. When the Babylonian empire invaded Judah, they took the smartest and best-looking Israelites as captives back with them to live as servants. Shadrach, Meshach, and Abednego were amongst the Israelites who lost their families, stature, homes, and possessions and were brought back to Babylon as slaves to work under the rule of king Nebuchadnezzar.

No good deed

During their captivity, the king established a new law. He brought his kingdom into an assembly and told them to kneel before and worship a newly construction idol made of gold. For the Israelites living as slaves in the Babylon empire, this new law was in direct opposition to the beliefs of the Jews and the Law of Moses. Informed that those who refused to comply with king Nebuchadnezzar's law would be thrown into a fiery furnace, Shadrach, Meshach, and Abednego chose to stand firm, refused to worship the idol, and resigned themselves to their promised fate.

When the king heard of their refusal, the three were brought before the king and given another opportunity to comply with this new decree. Instead, the three Hebrews, Shadrach, Meshach, and Abednego took a strong, public stand of faith, making it clear to the king and his kingdom that they understood their choice and would remain faithful to their God. King Nebuchadnezzar was furious with their betrayal, how dare did the captives dictate policy, he felt and ordered the furnace to be stoked up to seven times its usual level of heat. The three men were bound with ropes and thrown in. The Bible tells us the flames were so hot that the guards who brough them in were killed in the fire.

As the three Hebrews were tossed into the flames, King Nebuchadnezzar, wanted a better look at the torment of his disobedient captives so he bent down to look inside, expecting to see them men burning. Instead, the king witnessed the three men standing upright, unbound, and in a conversation with a fourth:

> *"Then King Nebuchadnezzar leaped to his feet in amazement and asked his advisers, "Weren't there three men that we tied up and threw into the fire?" They replied, "Certainly, Your Majesty." He said, "Look! I see four men walking around in the fire, unbound and unharmed, and the fourth looks like a son of the gods."* — Daniel 3:24-25 NIV

God is there too

God's presence was with them in the flames. As he spoke with Shadrach, Meshach, and Abednego, the fire did not touch their clothes, their skin, or the hairs on their heads. When king Nebuchadnezzar ordered them to come out of the fire, the Bible notes that even their clothes did not smell like smoke. His presence not only protected the three, but displayed the power of the one, true living God to those like king Nebuchadnezzar who had only known idols made of gold.

God came to these three in a very personal way, protecting them from the flames. What a lesson of hope this is for us! God is with us in the difficulties of our lives. He longs to be with us, and even in our darkest of days his presence is a promise we can cling to.

In What Ways Does God Prove He Cares About Me?

_____

_____

_____

_____

_____

_____

_____

_____

_____

_____

_____

_____

_____

_____

_____

_____

_____

He Gave It Up For You

"For you know the grace of our Lord Jesus Christ, that though he was rich, yet for your sake he became poor, so that you through his poverty might become rich." — II Corinthians 8:9 NIV

MAXIMILIAN KOLBE WAS a devout Franciscan Friar in Poland during the Nazi persecution and eventual invasion in 1941. He held a doctorate in Philosophy and publicly criticized the Nazi regime in Poland through his books and essays. To quiet Kolbe's voice, he was offered certain privileges in exchange for his silence. When Kolbe refused he was arrested, his monastery was shut down, and he was sent to the Auschwitz death camp, tattooed with the prisoner number 16670.

In July of 1941, ten prisoners escaped from the camp and to discourage any further attempts at escape, the Nazi guards selected ten prisoners to be sent to an underground bunker to be deprived of food or drink until they starved to death. One of the men chosen cried out that he had a wife and children. Kolbe stepped forward to take his place, and along with the nine others, was thrown into the bunker, left to die.

One of the men employed to clean the camp survived the war and spoke of Kolbe's story. He revealed that Kolbe led the condemned men in prayer, and lived two full weeks in the bunker, being the last of the prisoners to die. Kolbe did not die of starvation but was eventually given a lethal injection by the Nazi guards. The man whose life he saved lived to be 93 years old and dedicated much of his life to telling the world about Kolbe's actions and sacrifice on his behalf.

This incredible story causes us to think of the one who died on our behalf. Jesus laid aside his life for us. It was a choice that he willingly made, and a demonstration of God's heart toward us. Our restoration required a sacrifice, and instead of remaining far off, Jesus entered our human existence and experience to be that sacrifice and die in our place. Jesus came to earth to walk among us, like He as God did in Eden:

> *"But made himself of no reputation, and took upon him the form of a servant, and was made in the likeness of men: And being found in fashion as a man, he humbled*

*himself, and became obedient unto death,
even the death of the cross." — Phil
2:7-8 - NIV*

He removed his Power

The original Greek wording of these verses high-lights the personal choice God made to come to Earth, as it translates to mean that God removed His glory, as if taking it off a royal garment. He removed his glory and made himself to be nothing. He was born in a stable manger, among common people, and lived in Nazareth, a poor village that could be compared to a modern-day slum. Jesus entered the human experience with humility, making himself lowly. He was fully God, yet fully man, experiencing the same difficulties, emotions, and toil that we face, that we might related to him in all we are going through. The prophet Isaiah declares that the Savior born to us will be called "Immanuel," meaning God with us:

> *"The virgin will conceive and give birth to a son, and they will call him Immanuel"
> (which means "God with us").* —
> Mathew 1:23 NIV

God with us

Many of us are familiar with this idea from the Christmas hymn, but the translation of this term as a name for God is a stunning truth, and a promise we can cling to. "God with us." From the beginning of creation, God's intent has been to live among his people, having a close relationship with us. Even in the Garden of Eden, when man's decision put up a barrier and caused separation from God's presence, we see promises of the coming redemption and reconciliation to God through Jesus that would give us freedom and connection to him once again. God would come himself to redeem us:

> *"But God commends his love toward us, in that, while we were yet sinners, Christ died for us."* — Romans 5:8 NIV

Jesus knew the cost of our restoration, and he took it on willingly. He doesn't require that we clean ourselves up before accepting this offer of salvation and grace that is given through Christ. We are not able to live the perfect life without sin that is required to be in the presence of God. Like the pure and spotless atoning sacrifices of the Old Testament, Jesus is our pure and spotless sacrifice, dying in our place, He is the ultimate sacrifice, the one without sin who became sin on our behalf.

The night of Jesus' birth was without fanfare, a star in the sky, and a few angels to herald his birth. God came to us embracing the humble experience of humanity. After His birth, threats were being made upon his life and through a dream they were warned so Mary and Joseph escaped Nazareth and fled to Egypt. Several times through the life of Jesus, he faced persecution and threats of death. The Bible is clear that Jesus came to earth to die for us, and it was his resurrection that secures our salvation:

> *"None of the rulers of this age under-stood it, for if they had, they would not have crucified the Lord of glory." —*
> *I Corinthians 2:8 NIV*

Those who saw Jesus as a threat to their earthly power did not understand that Jesus' death and resurrection were part of God's sovereign plan. We are the reason God came. His life on earth was purposeful, and we were known by him when he chose to die for us. And now Jesus stands and the right hand of the Father, interceding on our behalf. He knows our names, and his death and resurrection cover our own, personal transgressions.

When Jesus speaks to the disciple known as Thomas He says:

*"Then Jesus told him, "Because you have seen
me, you have believed; blessed are those who
have not seen and yet have believed." —*
John 20:29 NIV

Here Jesus is referring to those believers who would
come after Thomas and the rest of those who had seen
him. When we trust Jesus, we embrace him as our Savior,
putting our faith in his death and resurrection as the
way to reconciliation with God. We embrace him as a
God who knows us and has sacrificed personally for us.

We may struggle with this offer of free grace, and
feel we are undeserving. We may believe we are not good
enough to accept this truth. My father was just such a
man. He watched myself, my sister and my mother put
our faith in Christ and begin attending church and getting involved. He saw the way this changed our family
dynamic and unbeknownst to us set up a meeting with
our minister to learn more.

Our pastor, Rev. Owen Carr was eager to share with
my father and explained in simple terms the love God
has for us. He told my father if he was serious about his
faith, he would need to make a public declaration of his
faith by coming forward on Sunday. My dad expressed
his desire to do so, but that he felt he needed to clean
up his life first to be acceptable to God first. Rev. Carr
explained to him that the gift of grace is offered freely.

> *"For it is by grace you have been saved,*
> *through faith—and this is not from*
> *yourselves, it is the gift of God."* —
> *Ephesians 2:8 NIV*

We can't do it alone

We may also feel unworthy of this gift, but we cannot redeem ourselves. Jesus has done the work on our behalf. All believers are a work in progress, letting the Holy Spirit do a transformative work in our lives as we grow in our faith and relationship with the Lord. People have tried following the laws of morality for centuries and have come up short. Our attempts at perfection will fail.

I remember believing as a child in a cosmic scoreboard that tallied up all my good and bad deeds. I thought when I did that if the good outweighed the bad, I would get to Heaven. How deceived I was like a dog chasing its tail, this idea earning, or restoration leads to exhaustion, and never reaching the goal we set out to attain. I would always come up short, until God entered my life. It is only through the gift of grace in Christ Jesus that we can receive salvation.

In What Ways Does God Prove He Cares About Me

_____

_____

_____

_____

_____

_____

_____

_____

_____

_____

_____

_____

_____

_____

_____

_____

_____

God is on Our Side

"Relent, Lord! How long will it be? Have compassion on your servants." — Psalm 90:13 NIV

As WE READ through the Old Testament we are captivated by and frequently frustrated with the story of the nation of Israel. The narrative tells us time and time again of the ways they veer off course and sin against God. Through the years of history recorded in the Bible, we see their repeated sins and failures captured in two main ways: their constant fear that God could not provide, and their tendency to turn and worship a creation of man or idea of success. We find a record of Israel's distrust and decision to turn from God:

> *"They did not keep God's covenant and refused to live by his law. They forgot what he had done, the wonders he had shown*

them. He did miracles in the sight of their ancestors in the land of Egypt, in the region of Zoan. He divided the sea and led them through; he made the water stand up like a wall. He guided them with the cloud by day and with light from the fire all night. He split the rocks in the wilderness and gave them water as abundant as the seas; he brought streams out of a rocky crag and made water flow down like rivers. But they continued to sin against him, rebelling in the wilderness against the Most High. They willfully put God to the test by demanding the food they craved. They spoke against God; they said, "Can God really spread a table in the wilderness? True, he struck the rock, and water gushed out, and streams flowed abundantly, but can he also give us bread? Can he supply meat for his people?" When the Lord heard them, he was furious; his fire broke out against Jacob, and his wrath rose against Israel, for they did not believe in God or trust in his deliverance. Yet he gave a command to the skies above and opened the doors of the heavens." —
Psalm 78:10-23 NIV

Israel's pattern of sin is often followed by judgement coming upon them. They are conquered time and again by rival nations and taken into captivity because of their disobedience. The nation would then repent and turns back to God, but eventually the cycle would begin again. Israel wasn't alone in this practice. The apostle Paul saw this repeating pattern in his day as well, and states in the book of the Acts of the Apostles:

> *"People of Athens! I see that in every way you are very religious. For as I walked around and looked carefully at your objects of worship, I even found an altar with this inscription: to an unknown god."* — Acts 17:22-23 NIV

Often, we see two words in association with their eventual freedom, "they repented" and, "God relented". To relent means to "to mitigate a harsh condition," according to the Google dictionary.

God changed His plan

> *"And God sent an angel to destroy Jerusalem. But as the angel was doing so, the Lord saw it and <u>relented</u> concerning the disaster and said to the angel who was destroying the*

people, "Enough! Withdraw your hand." —
II Samuel 24:16 NIV

And when King David stopped violating God's command, he made a sacrifice, God forgave them. It was reminder that God watches us intently. He is a very personal God who is interested in our affairs. What we do and why we do it are very important too God. As we have seen by the Israelites at Mt. Horeb their reaction showed that some will be put off by that kind of knowledge, while others will see it as it is, God cares.

God is on our side

He relents because he gets no pleasure out of punishment. As it is written:

> *"You do not delight in sacrifice, or I would bring it; you do not take pleasure in burnt offerings." — Psalm 51:16 NIV*

Just because God has opened a way for restoration, doesn't mean sacrifices are God's first choice. He would prefer we do it right in the first place. From God's perspective the sacrifice is like a good news/bad news joke. The Good News is that God will accept a sacrifice, the Bad news is we had to offer a sacrifice in the first place. It's like how we might feel about the medical field. They

36

are great with treatment, but not so good about prevention. We tend to rely on the sacrifice versus doing it right in the first place. We try to be nicer, make bigger donations, volunteer. But they are all secondary to what God prefers. He happily accepts them, but he would prefer our gifts be in the right place from the start, not some guilt motivated payment.

His willingness to turn from the wrath that we deserve, is again proof that God Loves us. He had to deal with Adam and Eve as they formed the first family. They had their own brand of dysfunction with their sons. They started it when they had disobeyed God by trusting in the words of another instead of the Creator. Then the one brother murders the other. God had not even written the Ten Commandments in stone with His finger yet, when God had to deal with it. What seemed logical to anyone else, "thou shalt not commit murder," had to be written down. Oh, my what a mess.

At some point in our lives, we probably have changed our mind, although we would prefer if others would change their mind.. When the Harvard Business Review was doing research for a book, they asked business leaders about their strategy to win someone over. Their best conclusion was, not to jump in and try to convince the other person. But invest time to personally learn about them and build rapport.

Notice that their survey found that it was a key component that someone takes the time to personally learn about those who will be impacted first before we act. Kind of like the adage of, "walking a mile in someone else's moccasins." That is exactly the strategy that God uses. God takes the time to learn about people and then He can relent and turn from His plan of judgement.

Noah was an exercise in patience

Consider how He dealt with Noah's world. Why would he destroy virtually every living thing all of which He created? Why didn't He relent then? Because He took the time to know his creation, he had delayed the flood for 100 years. During that time, it is obvious that Noah was constructing the Ark, but the Bible also teaches us that Noah preached to the people. He gave them ever opportunity to turn around. People chose to turn a deaf ear to the warnings. So that in his own words he spoke judgement by saying,

> *"The Lord saw how great the wickedness of the human race had become on the earth, and that every inclination of the thoughts of the human heart was only evil all the time. The Lord regretted that he had made human beings on the earth, and his heart was deeply troubled."* — Genesis 6:5-6 NIV

He had regret because He knew man's, "inclination was only evil...all the time." He was personal. Keep in mind regret is not the same as relent. We can see the tears streaming down the cheeks of a murderer. Sure, he has regrets for the action, but it is more that he got caught. What about the people he harmed, what about their tears? He changed their hearts forever and how can I empathize with him. To relent is tantamount to saying, "I regret." There is a sadness about it. That is our opportunity to appeal to God. It is our chance to put the past behind us and lean on Jesus.

He may yet relent

He provides to us an owner/operator instruction manual, but we chose to disregard it, then we wonder why we are in the trouble we are in, blaming ourselves, blaming others and even blaming God. When people ask, "why is there evil in the world," they don't get it, our stubborn determination to do our thing at no matter what the cost is the price we pay? But that is our plight. Each day we have a choice to turn to God and let Him bathe you in His sunshine. He may relent and override the consequences due us or He will let us ride it out knowing that a God who loves us is there by our side. Ever knocking at the door of our heart, He bids us to open and let Him in.

Consider the answer to Solomon at the dedication of the temple, amidst all the glorious decadence of that day when God is focused on one thing, He promised His willingness to relent and renew.

> *"If my people, who are called by my name, will humble themselves and pray and seek my face and turn from their wicked ways, then I will hear from heaven, and I will forgive their sin and will heal their land."*
> — II Chronicles 7:14 NIV

He opens his words with our responsibility, "if my people will humble themselves…" In other words, if we in our arrogance, admit we don't have all the answers, that is this first step toward recovery. But until we admit we don't have all answers, we are dead in the water and get to be the captain of our ship. We have to say we tried and were found waiting in our own strength. We must empty ourselves and rely on God. It may be the hardest thing to do in our life, letting go when every instinct tells us to tighten our grasp. But admitting our ability falls short is what we must do.

Paul had a thorn

We don't know what it was. Theories abound but the great apostle admits that he has one area of trouble

40

in his life. He had asked the Lord to take it away three times, to no avail. But God said know, this will be an area that will humble him, and the Apostle Paul puts his reaction it this way:

> *"…Therefore, I will boast even more gladly about my weaknesses, so that Christ's power may rest on me. That is why, for Christ's sake, I delight in weaknesses, in insults, in hardships, in persecutions, in difficulties. For when I am weak, then I am strong." — I Corinthians 12:9-10. NIV*

In our darkest moment, when healing doesn't come, our situation doesn't resolve, God has a plan to use us in unprecedented ways. How? We can't see it, but He does. Incredibly it will be specifically because of the difficulty and using our weakness to make it happen. Then no one can give us the credit, only God. How is that possible?

> *"But God chose the foolish things of the world to shame the wise; God chose the weak things of the world to shame the strong."* — I Corinthians 1:27 NIV.

In What Ways Does God Prove He Cares About Me?

_____

_____

_____

_____

_____

_____

_____

_____

_____

_____

_____

_____

_____

_____

_____

_____

_____

_____

God at Arm's Length

"Therefore, I will not keep silent; I will speak out in the anguish of my spirit, I will complain in the bitterness of my soul." — Job 7:11 NIV

WE FEEL UNCOMFORTABLE with close relationships and when they do happen, and it took a lot of work to get there. During one part of my life, I was offering my services as a minister to perform wedding officiating services for those who had no church home but wanted to include God on the guest list. I found it was a great to show young couples that not all Christians are crazy odd people, and that God could be relevant to their lives. I was surprised to learn from the couples that some ministers with whom they spoke required that they no longer live together for six weeks prior to the ceremony as if they could earn their way into heaven. I am not sure why the six-week abstinence period imposed on them was the magical amount or that they wouldn't find a way to sneak around the rule to get happy sometimes. They were already dealing with a lot of issues that if I presented to them the love of God that I might be able to help.

Wedding anniversary

On one day, we were all lined up preparing to enter the ballroom when the father of the groom came up to me and said, "Rev. Barry, I would like you to meet my parents who are celebrating their 60th anniversary today." I expressed a comment about how sweet that they will be sharing anniversaries with their young grandkids. Then I mentioned that I offer couple weeks to help them navigate their early years and at those seminars I am often asked the secret of a happy home. Since they have been together over 60 years, "How would they answer that question if it had been posed to them?" The husband without thought quickly responded, "Do whatever she says." And laughed knowingly at which his wife slapped his arm playfully.

There is some wisdom in that comment, going into marriage like any relationships means we must be willing to relinquish some degree of control. We recognize that to be truly happy we must surrender certain activities for the relationship to work. If we insist to not make those changes our relationship may be in jeopardy.

Imagine a groom telling his wife, "Honey, I love you, but I would like to continue seeing other another woman." That statement would not go over very well with our wife. She would begin to assume something must be wrong with her that would keep us looking at someone else or that we're are just being a creep who didn't take his vows seriously. Either way it devalues our position.

The pursuit of exclusivity

Yet we find Israel doing just that. And by denying an exclusive relationship with God we are doing essentially just that. We can't take the good, tasty aspects of Christianity and deny there is some responsibilities that go along with it. But that was what we find here. We want to keep God at arm's length. We minimize the relational aspects to keep our options open. We don't like the restrictive nature of commitment, we'd rather complain.

We complain about something until we get what we want or get a firm no. But according to one researcher on his blog post, complaining has a detrimental effect and is a bad habit. It will put all the parties in a bad mood. It keeps us focused on the flaws and problems. It annoys the people who must listen or makes them feel that they are incompetent and unhelpful. Complaining makes life feel like an ordeal instead of a gift, for both givers and receivers. The biggest problem with complaining is that it doesn't always get to the heart of the matter. The Children of Israel were famous for their oral traditions of complaint.

Complaints here

I think everyone is familiar with the cartoon asking us to write our presumably long complaint into a small square box provided on a form. It is telling the person our need is welcome, but only if we can fit it in here. It is funny unless we are serious about our concern. It feels like the issue should consume everybody else's time and isn't funny. I appreciated a quote from my boss when he was sharing his father's saying, "If every body's wrong and we alone are right, check our position." Certainly, we should be careful what we wish for because we might just get it. And that resulted into a tradition that lasted hundreds of years. God thought His plan was good, man thought he knew better.

We may be familiar with the prophets of the Bible, and depending on our source, there are 45 named prophets in the Bible and many more of whom we have never heard of in a sermon or Bible study because their impact was so minor. Some of the ones we may have heard of include names like Isaiah, Ezekiel, Daniel, and Jeremiah. Then there are lessor known prophets (minor prophets) like Obadiah and Jonah who are quoted when it is felt appropriate.

But here is some trivia for you, why God created the role of prophets in the first place? It is actually because of us and our preference of how we wanted to interact with God. It all dates to Mt Sinai and the story of Moses getting the Ten Commandments. There once again we find God's desire for intimacy with man. We see in the Garden of Eden before Adam and Eve rebelled against God. The Bible shows us how God interacted with Adam and Eve. There is no reference that God spent His time with the other beasts of the field. People were not just considered simply as sophisticated animals who had evolved into more complex creatures.

> *"Then the man and his wife heard the sound of the Lord God as he was walking in the garden in the cool of the day".* — Genesis 3:8 NIV

God used to be closer

We get a glimpse of how God spoke to man once upon a time. There is God walking on earth in the evening fully expecting to see Adam and Eve. In those days He just spoke Adam's name. He wanted to talk face to face. But sin meant He could not enjoy the presence physically of man ever again. He couldn't take a quiet stroll in the Garden without addressing the gorilla in the room. Something had changed. God knew it, Adam knew it, Eve knew it and the serpent knew it.

That was how it was. Now fast forward to the great mountain of Sinai. The occasion was recorded in Deuteronomy. We can hear God's delight when He brags about how lucky Israel were to have a personal relationship where He could talk directly to Humans again. He points, like a proud Father, to the other nations idols not being as close or receptive, after all they were items of man's creation using wood and stone. How that He had found a way to respond directly with humankind. But people thought differently.

> *"What other nation is so great as to have*
> *their gods near them the way the Lord our*
> *God is near us whenever we pray to him?*
> *And what other nation is so great as to have*
> *such righteous decrees and laws as this body*
> *of laws I am setting before you today?"* —
> Deuteronomy 4:7-8 NIV

We don't like feeling close to God

The people of Israel didn't feel comfortable with this direct close approach that God used. Afterall, He was the all-powerful Living God. He created all that we knew. He was invisible and when he spoke, great fire was seen, and the earth shook. He couldn't help it. His very presence was awe-inspiring. God wanted to keep the personal touch, intimacy with us, but man in fear of the special effects wanted an intermediary like themselves. A flawed plan, but one they felt would be easy on them. Sort of like having a person working on the inside. They preferred having someone that they could relate to instead of a relationship with power. So, they recommended we appoint people as intermediaries.

> *The Lord your God will raise up for you a prophet like me from among you, from your fellow Israelites. You must listen to him. For this is what you asked of the Lord your God at Horeb on the day of the assembly when you said, "Let us not hear the voice of the Lord our God nor see this great fire anymore, or we will die."*— Deuteronomy 18:15-16 NIV

God desired a more personal relationship, but at this time it was a "best practice" serving as a replacement. In other words, since the people who gathered at Mt. Sinai were too afraid of a face-to-face encounter, God was reluctantly willing to select someone from their people who can act as a conduit between God and man.

We got what we wanted, a more distant relationship with God. We were the original reason the office of prophet was introduced. We preferred keeping God at arm's length. We, us, made our choice known when our descendants said we would rather appoint a person and God speaks through them. As we can imagine this opened a myriad of problems for them and us today.

At best we hope the human element doesn't get in the way of the message, so we can understand God's directive. Or at worst some would seek to misuse the role of prophet for, their personal gain. Historically, the second was unfortunately truer than the first. We can understand some miscues by accident but to purposely misuse the power to enrich themselves, sounds terrible.

The game of telephone

Either way we are still playing the child's game of telephone. Interpreting positively or negatively what we believe to be true. With this information, it was at best what we had to work with because we preferred the blunder to the thunder. That is why we are in this predicament. We prefer it, we demand it, we abuse it. But we who are New Testament Christ followers, can take it another way. Instead of talking to our minister in a little room, today we can reach out to Him in the convenience of our space any time of day.

Just because the past was full of fear and trepidation doesn't mean our future traditions have to be that way. We can start a new tradition of prayer. Personally, speaking to God our most intimate of secrets. Tell him the truth and admitting our fears or our sins and need of His presence in our life. Begin today, open up and if we need to just cry don't worry, He has all the time in the world to wait and listen. How special is that intimate expression?

It is like the fragrance of the best incense in heaven. The aroma of our brokenness is literally what fills the throne room of God.

> *"The smoke of the incense, together with the prayers of God's people, went up before God from the angel's hand."* — Revelation 8:4 NIV

The incense is rising at this moment. It is holy in its substance and meaningful in its purpose. Our hurts or joys can be felt in heaven today. We can come to God without anyone else talking for us.

In What Ways Does God Prove He Cares About Me?

_____

_____

_____

_____

_____

_____

_____

_____

_____

_____

_____

_____

_____

_____

_____

I Can't Take It Anymore

"But if from there you seek the Lord your God, you will find him if you seek him with all your heart and with all your soul." — Deuteronomy 4:29 NIV

HAVE YOU BEEN there? Maybe we're there now. The world is crashing in around us and we wished we had never been born. It was the pivotal moment in the classic movie, "It's a Wonderful Life." George Bailey had a strange turn of events that put him in the crosshairs of the IRS through no fault of his own. He ends up on the bridge of a nearby river during a snowstorm, very symbolic of the collapse of his life, saying he wished he had never been born. His prayer was granted along with the guide of his guardian angel, Clarence. While it is a fictional tale, we have all been there at one time or another when we have fallen victim to the world around us.

Even big prophets were depressed

One of the flashiest prophets of the Old Testament knows, His name is Elijah. He had just come off a great victory. We don't think of it that way, but it is our most susceptible times, when we are on top of the world. We can make some risky and some not so smart decisions because we have a sense of being invulnerable. Kind of like the quote "believing their own press reports." We think we are smarter than we are. So, we may act a little cocky with the bravado we are feeling. It can be reflected in the way we treat others even ourselves.

Elijah had a great deal of faith and confidence that God would come through. And come through he did according to Elijah when God's reputation was on the line, but he was unable to muster up faith when he dealt with a personal attack. That may be true for us as well. We can believe God for big things, but we shrink back thinking God doesn't care about our individual situation or that my needs are inconsequential or that we deserve to suffer because of our choices. It couldn't be farther from the truth.

Consider this we do have to deal with the consequences of our decisions, no question. However, God understands that we are still fallible. We are not perfect. No surprise there. We don't fully understand the end game and we will make mistakes and hopefully avoiding repeats of our past mistakes. But sometimes we are just too thick headed to get it. God still forgives us. If we come to Him and humbly admit our wrongs and turn to Him. Acknowledge our inadequacies and He will reach out to us, it is a very personal matter.

We are most vulnerable on the heels of success

Elijah was drinking in his triumph over the false prophets when queen Jezebel focuses her hate on him and threatens that he will be dead within 24-hours, or her name isn't queen Jezebel. So tough was her threat that to this day the name Jezebel is associated with a floozie. She is so sure in her edict's success that she pro-claims it will be carried out her timeline. It was specific enough that Elijah ran for his life.

With this news we find this great prophet of God on the run. He could trust God to a point, but it had a limit. He trusted God with an exposition head-to-head with the false prophets and their claims. But to have his life threatened meant he had no faith. It was too per-sonal. Too close to home.

Do we have areas of our life that are simple for us to believe God for help and yet we have other areas we really struggle? We can pray for others, but to pray for ourself is hard. It is funny how we can be so alike the great people of God. In the New Testament there is a story of a centurion coming to Jesus and appealing for his son's life who is gravely ill. I love the admission of the centurion pleading for the life of his son to Jesus. I have had to quote it often when talking to God about my needs. There is a level of faith we all have and sometimes it comes up short. With all the honesty this father could muster up on behalf of his son he proclaims simply when he was questioned about the level of faith he had,

> *"Immediately the boy's father exclaimed, "I do believe; help me overcome my unbelief!"*
> — Mark 9:24 NIV

Honesty with God

It is with beautiful honesty that he spoke with Jesus. We can be honest with God, He can take it, in fact He welcomes it. The result was as we can imagine, health for his son. What keeps us from this simple declaration? There is no shame in admitting our short falls, we all have them. The shame is not admitting our inadequacies and pretending we are untouchably perfect.

In the test with the prophet, it was extravagant and totally dependent on the Lord. Elijah claimed that he could call down fire from the heavens and consume the gathered wood, but their false gods would be powerless to accomplish the same contest. Sure, enough the false prophets danced and gyrated but to no avail. So pathetic was the display of human invention that at one point Elijah shouted out the reason for the failure was, their god might be on the toilet or the reason that the gods didn't hear them was they were busy elsewhere. He taunted them mercilessly.

Now it was Elijah's turn to answer his critics. So confident he was in God that he told them to first soak the wood with water. It was the first glimpse of vanity on the part of Elijah. His first tarnish that led to the eventual threats he would face. While on first glance it would appear that he was full of faith. But consuming the wood with fire would have been enough to prove God was real. To add water to make it more difficult was his ego's attempt to show off. He was trying to make a grandiose display of his access to the power of God. Something he would pay for when the queen later threatens his life. It lowered God to the level of a servant or that Elijah was a magician.

It is a cautionary tale that exposes Elijah's efforts to the level of a trickster. He makes a scene that shows God answering to Elijah, lowering God to that of a genie in the lamp like the Arabian Nights tale of Aladdin. Make no mistake we must realize there is also the sovereignty of God at work that needs to be considered when making our requests. God answer's every prayer, but we don't know what God has in mind when He answers a prayer with a "yes," and when He answers with a "no."

The sword of Damocles

In Cicero's story of the sword of Damocles which is often quoted by people meaning we are living in imminent danger who have such power. According to the story, Damocles worked in the court of the king Dionysus one day he was pandering to his king, exclaiming how he was so fortunate to work for such a great man of power and authority without peer. In response, Dionysius offered to switch places with Damocles for one day so that Damocles could taste that very fortune firsthand. Damocles quickly and eagerly accepted the king's proposal.

When Damocles sat on the king's throne, he was surrounded by countless luxuries. But Dionysius, had made many enemies during his reign, and so he had arranged that a sword should hang above the throne, held only by a single hair of a horse's tail. To remind him always of what it is like to be king: though having much fortune, he was having to watch in fear and anxiety against dangers that might try to overtake him. When he discovered the hanging sword, Damocles begged the king that he be allowed to depart because he no longer wanted to be so fortunate, realizing that with great fortune and power comes also great danger.

There is a danger with power

This is the risk of letting vanity govern our decisions. We enjoy the blessings of God one day but realize it can all disappear quickly the next day. In a moment we can go from the king of our domain to a pauper begging in the court.

So, the false prophets did soak the wood pile according to the instructions and the undoing of Elijah began to start. Not evident at first, it seemed like victory or success was at the doorstep. But his vanity was insatiable so Elijah called for another dowsing of water to make sure no one could claim the demonstration was rigged. His vanity is not satisfied so he asks them to soak the wood a second and third time. No one at the assembly understood, and many Christians fail to recognize the mistake Elijah had done. So true is the problem of vanity, we don't recognize the symptoms until it is too late. The trap is set. And with that Elijah called to God and instantly fire from heaven came down and burned up the wood.

Moses was angry

Even the famed Moses and the story of Israel arriving at the promised land wasn't exempt from the impact of vanity. For forty years they had highs and lows, but Moses was the steady one until he let his ego get in the way. Yet he faced a result of his actions that disqualified him from entering the promised land like everyone else.

The people were complaining to him again about needing water. God specifically told Moses to speak to a certain rock and water would gush forth providing the people with life giving water. Instead, we find Moses letting his emotions get the best of him by striking the rock and releasing the water, making it seem like his power brought the water, instead of God.

It wasn't the first time we see his emotion get the best of him. In his early years he killed an Egyptian he saw beating a Hebrew slave and even when he came down the mountain with the original Ten Commandments and found the people had given up on him and so he hurtled the tablets down that God had carved out which necessitated him to chisel out his own copy.

Elijah's faith in God seemed verified, when God sent down fire, but then came the queen's rage. The fear of the situation became overwhelming. Something was wrong. Why didn't the story end with success and a lesson to trust in a faithful God? Instead, Elijah took off running in fear of his life. In fact, Elijah wanted to put as much distance between queen Jezebel and himself as possible. So, like "*Forrest Gump*," he just ran.

The Bible says he ran for twenty-four hours. He didn't eat, he didn't sleep, he just ran until the point of exhaustion. We find him going from the glory days of fire coming down from heaven and consuming the waterlogged wood, to emptiness of heart sitting under a broom bush, curled up at the lowest part of his life asking God to take it, for he wished he had never been born, just like George Bailey in "*It's a Wonderful Life.*"

> "*Elijah was afraid and ran for his life. When he came to Beersheba in Judah, he left his servant there, while he himself went a day's journey into the wilderness. He came to a broom bush, sat down under it and prayed that he might die. "I have had enough, Lord," he said. "Take my life; I am no better than my ancestors." Then he lay down under the bush and fell asleep.*" —
> I Kings 19:3-5 NIV

We are so hypocritical

While he slept an angel cooked him a meal and when Elijah woke up, he ate and began his spiritual journey back to God. How could he be full of faith one minute and so desperate the next? That is the human condition. We are full of contradictions. On top of the world one moment and in the basement the next. He literally had a death wish when earlier God had just shown His amazing power, He had simply done hours earlier. Granted he had no sleep or rest, anxious and starving. Being in a weakened state did him no favors, we should take the lesson to heart.

But what happens next is incredible. He eats the supernaturally prepared meal and in answer to prayer, God sends an earthquake, while Elijah thought okay God, He has the power to snuff out my enemies, but it ended with just an earth-shaking moment. Then God sends a lightning bolt, kind of like what we ask for from time to time. Then comes a howling wind.

Each time Elijah expected an extravagant message from God. Something grandiose and stupendous, to the level of consuming the drenched firewood. But God was in none of it. He was working with Elijah on a need basis. Instead, the personal God that He is, instead sends His comforting words that were just a whispered voice. Something that many of us never hear.

> *"Then a great and powerful wind tore the mountains apart and shattered the rocks before the Lord, but the Lord was not in the wind. After the wind there was an earthquake, but the Lord was not in the earthquake. After the earthquake came a fire, but the Lord was not in the fire. And after the fire came a gentle whisper."* — Kings 19:11-12 NIV

God is speaking to us, and we may expect a loud and audacious event when He knows what we need is simply a quiet whisper of assurance. It is kind of like when my wife says I need to stop trying to solve her problems and just listen to her bear her soul. I think in rescue terms when she just needs to be valued. She explains she is not looking for solutions, she can find them a dime a dozen. But looking for understanding and a feeling like she is valued and not alone is important. He will speak to us based on our need and with both, the crashing thunder, or the whisper. Just keep listening.

Talk too much

We all know people who "talk too much." They go on and on monopolizing the conversation. We sit there waiting for an opportunity to voice our opinion, but it's hard to get a word in edge wise, so we wait. The longer they go on talking the more we must work to hold on to our thought. Sooner or later, we spend so much time and effort holding on to our thought we are no longer listening. By doing that we are eliminating input from others that might radically help change our viewpoint.

Control

Psychologists know the monopolizing of the conversation, as well-meaning as it appears on the forefront, is a coping mechanism that is all about control. By talking incessantly, we control the floor, and we are safe. If we are talking and sharing our opinion, we don't have to listen to another person who might express a differing opinion and the controller might be proven wrong. We don't have to accept the truth that we might not know all the facts. So, oblivious to the dynamics of what is going on, subconsciously, some people continue to talk.

It is hard to believe we're guilty of the same thing with God, even when we say we pray. We are just stating our requests. It is a litany of statements meant to demonstrate our competency of the issue being discussed. There is nothing wrong with intercession, but not all the time. Sometimes we may find God just sitting around the corner waiting for us to finish asking.

Christ followers can be making the same mistake and with good intentions. Have we thought about just sitting there quietly in God's Presence and listening for him to direct our life or adjust our prospective? At least we've thought about being quiet. But we are so used to telling our side of the story compete with validation of how awesome we are, we literally can't stop ourself.

We can't hear God

Most know what the term, "meditation" means and even then, misapply it. We sit there with soft music playing in our ears and call it our time waiting on God.

Hey, our music may be too loud to hear a whisper from God. There is nothing wrong with music its great on the treadmill. But don't confuse the "beat" of the music with meditation. Don't confuse the idea that if we can dance to it, we're spending time with God.

Elijah got a bit confused with the sounds he heard. He was expecting God to speak with tones of grand majesty. But instead, God sent a gentle whisper like a loving parent to his wounded child. If Elijah wasn't listening or open, he might have missed it. The very thing he needed from God.

Might I suggest that all of us could be reminded to pause in our life and in quietness sit there and stop talking for once. We might find that to talk incessantly is to be holding only one half of the conversation with the King of Glory. He wants to comfort us, may be even tell us His plans, but we're too busy to be talking to hear them. Stop and listen, we might be surprised at what we hear.

We may be looking for the wrong message

We expect God to hear a loud booming voice when He plans to simply talk to us. The past may contain displays of the great successes we've have had with God. We may have been surrounded with faith, but it isn't over. There are new challenges to face. Do not rely on the past to get us through. We need a fresh dose of faith to meet the future.

Elijah's story is one of great victory but when we start to take credit and vanity creeps in, be reminded of this story as we may find ourself humbly beneath a broom bush.

> *"Because of the Lord's great love, we are not consumed, for his compassions never fail. They are new every morning. Great is your faithfulness."* — Lamentations 3:22-23 NIV

God does feel every pain we are experiencing whether it's our family, or emotional, or mental or physical or all of the above. He is not low in His inventory of compassion as is promised in the preceding verses. Every day there is new batch and supply. God will send us what we need.

In What Ways Does God Prove He Cares About Me?

_____

_____

_____

_____

_____

_____

_____

_____

_____

_____

_____

_____

_____

_____

_____

_____

_____

He Chose Us

"As Jesus was walking beside the Sea of Galilee, he saw two brothers, Simon called Peter and his brother Andrew. They were casting a net into the lake, for they were fishermen. 'Come, follow me,' Jesus said, "and I will send you out to fish for people." At once they left their nets and followed him."
— Matthew 4:18-20 NIV

I REMEMBER THE feeling as it happened repeatedly when I was a child and youth. We were picking teams. We lined up, side by side with two people selecting their teams. Most often they would first select the biggest and strongest, then the chosen were among those that were considered the most skilled in a position. Then there was me being clearly and reluctantly selected. They didn't hide their feelings about having to pick among the "remaining losers."

Those who had been selected stood around their teammates and were celebratory at first. But as the selection and popularity of the remaining players dwindled so to the joyful optimism diminished. Sometimes I was just waved over to my teammates instead of called by name. It was a real ego buster. As an adult my softball coach rarely let me play. One time he explained how much he liked having me on the team, I perked up, but then he went on to explain his reason for joy in having me on the team was that I never complained about sitting on the bench. Sort of a backhanded compliment. My value was in being quiet.

When selecting His disciples, we might be tempted to say, "yah, yah, let's get on to the miracles of Jesus," we might miss the profound truth of the moment. He handpicked each disciple with care. Jesus didn't just stand up in front of a crowd and ask for volunteers. He didn't build a team from those selected by management. He reached out to each one of those early disciples with care and future purpose in mind. Sometimes that got Him in trouble with the religious leaders who had a certain type in their mind which they thought should be among His followers. They wanted to put the Jesus followers in a box. But that never got in Jesus' way, He had another type in mind. He was very careful to pick the first missionaries, because he knew they would face not only hardships, but persecutions that would test their faith.

He chose us

In other words, He chose the poor people, the common people and the rich independently and personally. Knowing the future that lay ahead was important. The plan had been millenniums in the making. It was critical He would choose the right people to carry the message forward. He was not looking for simpletons but critical thinkers. People who approach life like us. Those who didn't just take things at face value. It isn't surprising to find tradition telling us that all but John were martyred for their faith. They were hard core "show me people." He knew what they would face in the years ahead. Intense persecution, challenging their very fundamentals.

Peter needed to be tough as the first church leader, so He picked a hardened fisherman who knew despite the weather he would go out and fish anyway. As we read about his exploits, we see this tough guy was also quick to draw a sword. From the beginning Jesus saw something special in Peter that would propel the church, he saw potential in him. While others feared for their lives on a stormy sea, it was Peter who walked on water to meet Jesus, sounds like Jesus made a good choice. He also had some unpolished sides to him, but he was still chosen.

Then there was Thomas who demanded proof of the resurrection, not just wishful thinking. We benefitted from his hard headedness, and demand of physical proof. To bolster our faith he vetted the truth of the resurrection of Jesus which is cited to this day. Luke was a physician and went into detail when it came to the healing miracles of Jesus. Thanks to him we understand that the stories of the sick being set free are confirmed by a doctor and not just accept by faith.

We see He chose them very carefully whether they realized it or not. Let's face it much of the pain and joy of our life was caused by the people we choose to associate ourselves with. What do we use as criteria of the people we choose to be an influence in our life? As one motivational speaker points out, "we are the average of the five people we spend the most time with." Of course, we immediately think of the bad influences first or at least I do, but it works the other way around too. The positive voices give us support and hope. They can offer so much faith in one area of our life that it spills over into another area of life.

Julie and I attend a weekly small group and they shape me. Each week their generosity and support are there to make us stronger. Our group is also a very strong prayer group. Each week we pull each other over the finish line. We purposefully work that faith building into our study.

We can't understand everything

If Jesus was so careful, why did He pick a denier? Because that is also our story, our life that includes doubt. It is amazing we have faith in something we can't touch at all. In the same way, we have denied Jesus claims on our life over and over. Through our trust and lack of faith we are guilty of hiding in the corner hearing the words of accusation by a servant girl.

Jesus knew this dark time of Peter's time was coming and wanted him to know in advance and not let him be surprised and then discouraged by his own denials. Not just one moment of fear. But Peter had an important trust needed to be built. So, he had three separate denials. God understands that we are looking through what the apostle Paul calls a "glass darkly." That what we understand and see is only a partial if not distorted image of the world as He sees it. We can be so convinced in our truth and be dead wrong. Peter promises he will never deny but will only defend Jesus, and when he does so to add further insult to injury it is punctuated with the sound of a crow in the distance letting out a cry. Peter was decimated as he heard the crow of the rooster as Jesus predicted.

God cares

As terrible and surprising as Peter's denial is to these events, God didn't forget Peter. As confirmed on the morning of Jesus resurrection when the angel told the women to go tell the others that Jesus came back from the dead. The news was joyous enough, yet the angel called out to the women who were leaving to share the first missionary story. Out of deep concern, the angel stopped the women. He gave them specific instructions, to find the distraught Peter and to make sure he knew it was okay. I can't imagine how the impulsive, tough Peter took the news. He was singled out on his boat with fishnets at his feet now on this day once again he singled out with words He is risen.

> *"But go, tell his disciples and Peter, 'He is going ahead of you into Galilee. There you will see him, just as he told you.'"*— *Mark 16:7*

It was a very careful and personal, "It's okay" for Peter, from Jesus. While everyone would be delighted to hear of the resurrection, to Peter it had a special meeting. It meant all was forgiven. Not that God forgot. But that God remembered and forgave while not needing to bring up again. Not just his sin, but his denial. Perhaps it was even part of the plan.

We may have denied Christ access into the various rooms of our heart in so many ways. But remember He arose; he is at the right hand of the Father speaking on our behalf. Advocating for our forgiveness, understanding our struggle today to trust Him. The right hand was more than a seat of honor, it was a place of ultimate trust and power. It signified the authority of the Father.

> *"And he who searches our hearts knows the mind of the Spirit, because the Spirit intercedes for God's people in accordance with the will of God."— Romans 8:27 NIV*

From that place of honor, we find Jesus saying our name. Not like a guest's name is introduced at a gala at the ballroom entrance, but as stating "let him go, he's mine," in a courtroom. There are many jokes that begin with Peter at the Pearly Gates. But it is God's own son who speaks out on our behalf. And that is no joke.

Our name can be in the book of life

Our surrender today puts our name on the list. Trust Jesus with our heart and we will experience what it will be like to be among the chosen. Of course, there will be days when we surrender to the cares of this world, ask Peter about bad days, but Sunday is coming. With that tomorrow's sunrise we not only face a new day we are a new person. Like a caterpillar becomes a butterfly so we will undergo a metamorphosis, transformation. Our interests and values can be changed or embolden. The Bible tells us about that change when it says ...

> *"Therefore, if anyone is in Christ, the new creation has come: The old has gone, the new is here!"* — 2 Corinthians 5:17

In What Ways Does God Prove He Cares About Me?

_____

_____

_____

_____

_____

_____

_____

_____

_____

_____

_____

_____

_____

_____

_____

_____

_____

Of Every Nation

"When he saw the crowds, he had compassion on them, because they were harassed and helpless, like sheep without a shepherd."
— *Matthew 9:36 NIV*

OVER THE YEARS I have spent a lot of time in shopping malls, when that was place for large scale commerce and transactions. It is hard to imagine there was a time when the shopping mall was the center point of society with its activity as we walk in them now. But it was a bustling place of activity, and I would find it a great location to study, or read, and people watch. It was fun to watch the people pass by the thousands both rich and poor.

But Jesus saw people differently. He was like a human x-ray machine with legs and could see right through them to their heart. Take one occasion when He spoke to a woman drawing water from a well. It was a simple task and not too different from going to the shopping mall. The watering wells were open at the time and were a gathering place for people to socialize, get their water, hear the latest gossip, and return home.

My first assignment as a youth minister was rather deflating of my ego. I joined the pastoral team thinking of all the fun things I would do, more like a camp counselor than associate pastor. But the lead minister saw me as a young man who needed pastoral experience, and he was right. No sooner had I arrived in town, he asked me to accompany him on visitation. We got in his car and drove just a short distance to a house that had all the shades drawn. We knocked on the door and we were ushered in to a home with quiet tones.

She was in a coma

The mother of the house was comatose and was kept in a hospital bed in the side room off the kitchen. After we exchanged a few pleasantries with her husband, he took us to the bedside of her prepared room. She was tossing around, but it was soon replaced with a supernatural calm when the pastor prayed. The moment he finished praying the violent bouncing returned. They didn't teach us this is seminary. When we returned to the car, he told me this was my first assignment, he asked me to visit this family every day.

I was moved by what I had just experienced much as Jesus must have been moved when He looked at people. When He was here, He experienced every loss felt by every person. But this day was far from ordinary. Her conversation was normal at first, but Jesus got personal, looking into her soul, and seeing what was really happening, her response was utter shock. He spoke to her, shattering the glass of the racial and gender ceiling.

A Samaritan, whom Jews had no deals, because they were largely made up a mixed race comprised of Hebrews and those who lived in Samaria. Then He revealed an intimate knowledge about her life choices. It was a shock that He spoke to her back in those days, but don't get too hung up by the fact she was a woman. More importantly was that He had never met her previously, yet knew every intimate detail of her life. That was what impressed her most.

> *"Come, see a man who told me everything I ever did. Could this be the Messiah?"* — John 4:29 NIV

It is important to describe the situation more fully in which Moses wrote the first five books of the Bible. The children of Israel were initially led into Egypt by Joseph as a shelter from the drought 430 years earlier. Eventually a new pharaoh came on the scene who did not know Joseph and so he took all these Hebrew people living in Egypt and turned them into slaves. When Moses at 80 years of age came asking Pharoah to release the Hebrews from slavery it was a major economic disaster to the nation. But the plagues were worse, and Pharoah reluctantly released the Hebrews from slavery, and they left in mass and the people began their 40-year exodus in the desert.

Racial diversity was protected

They had no policies, no laws, no Bill of Rights or rules or Constitution as a nation to govern them. So Moses wrote many laws to set priorities which became the first legal documents of the newly freed people. In them contained a law of inclusion that eventually became perverted by future governments:

> *"The foreigner residing among you must be treated as your native-born. Love them as yourself, for you were foreigners in Egypt. I am the Lord your God."* — Deuteronomy 19:34 NIV

Jesus' work with the woman at the well was proof that God came for every man, woman, and child of all colors. From the very beginning He accepts people of all races. There is no subjugation, no curse. The Gospel is freely available to all who come to Jesus. While some races claim to hold the corner of the market to share the "truth" in the Bible they preach it is not open to all races, but God is against favoritism of any kind.

> "*For God does not show favoritism.*" — Romans 2:11 NIV

Even a careful examination of the day of Pentecost after Jesus resurrection when the Holy Spirit is poured out on all who were present. In a general comment Luke writes:

> "*Now there were staying in Jerusalem God-fearing Jews from every nation under heaven…*" — *Acts 2:5 NIV*

Every nation

Note that the broad outpouring that Luke records goes on to list at least 16 nations were named as being in the crowd. The Jews that still celebrate this day calling it, "Shavuot" and claim there may be upwards of 70 nations represented there for that day of celebration. Either number shows there was a lot of racial inclusion in this supernatural event by God. He doesn't discriminate by cultures, beliefs, or color of skin. That is God's dream plan spoken of in Revelation, that people of all types are gathered for worship. It reads:

> *"After this I looked, and there before me*
> *was a great multitude that no one could*
> *count, from every nation, tribe, people and*
> *language, standing before the throne and*
> *before the Lamb. They were wearing white*
> *robes and were holding palm branches in*
> *their hands."* — Revelation 7:9 NIV

This inclusion is further highlighted when the Prophet Samuel was selecting the next king of Israel. Samuel stood face to face with each of Jesse's sons to select the next king, but he came away empty handed. When he asked their father if this were all the children, he admits there is one more. Left alone, David was watching the sheep while the others were there to present themselves. The one missing, was the youngest boy, but God couldn't be interested in him. The father questioned the prophet Samuel as to his selection process as he saw only his version of what it will take to be the next king. He saw David as being too young and inexperienced, however, Samuel shared how God sees people:

> *"But the Lord said to Samuel, 'Do not con-*
> *sider his appearance or his height, for I have*
> *rejected him. The Lord does not look at the*
> *things people look at. People look at the*

*outward appearance, but the Lord looks at
the heart.'"* — I Samuel 16:7 NIV

It is also important to note that God knows all
about us. He knows everything, and He still loves us.
He hears thousands of voices speaking the intents of
the heart and relaying the actions each person. One of
my personal favorite verses in the Bible reads,

> *"You see, at just the right time, when we
> were still powerless, Christ died for the
> ungodly. Very rarely will anyone die for a
> righteous person, though for a good person
> someone might possibly dare to die. But
> God demonstrates his own love for us in
> this: While we were still sinners, Christ
> died for us."* — *Romans 5:6-8 NIV*

He accepts us the way we are

I find it incredible to think He knew the kind of
people we are and willingly gave His life anyway. When
we weren't so nice, He made the decision to love us still.
God still sees our potential. In whatever condition we
are in He accepts us because we can't save ourself.

But that brings us back to a certain day in the spring
and the launch of a glorious week, this day was special.
He has been leading a parade of people. Not because He

was ego driven, because they had their needs met. The ranks of followers burgeoned as he moved along. It was a celebration, to the people, perhaps an Independence Day from Rome. Branches were stripped from trees were laid out in front of Him as He traveled. Robes were strewn to cover the ground. Jesus tolerated their excitement.

They rose to the crest of the hill overlooking Jerusalem and when He saw the city, He stopped the mule He was riding. And He heard a thousand souls cry out. Without one voice heard over another He heard the city with an intimate cry of the need of salvation, shouting to the One who could help them.

> *"As he approached Jerusalem and saw the city, he wept over it"* — Luke 19:41 NIV

He weeps for our needs

It was a reminder to us and me that God cares and hears us in our hour of desperation. For those of us that say "My life is fine, I am not desperate I would say either you are self-diluted, or you are in a good place but one day you'll wish Jesus would have His arms wrapped around us weeping with us.

One University expressed their concern about cities when they wrote, that our society is moving at a fast pace and as it does its citizens will become increasingly detached from each other due to advances in technology, busy schedules, and the frequency at which we move and change jobs, making it harder and harder to feel a sense of community. We will not be able to hear the cries of need because we are too self-absorbed.

Trying to understand how God sees cities is to understand that he sees a community of people, not stores and offices. A city is not simply a collection of manufacturers, retail outlets or food sources. We are a community first and merchant second. If we lead with our self-inflicted frantic pace, we have lost a key element of who we are.

The next time we see a crowd we may be at the airport terminal or a sporting event. We may be at the shopping mall, just remember Jesus couldn't go to them without hearing the voices of souls calling to Him. He cares intimately for us.

He knows all that we've have done and understands, as well as what has been done to us. Without judgement He accepts us as we are in this space and time. Broken limbs or broken hearts, won't you let Him in?

There is a small book by Robert Boyd Munger, entitled, "My Heart, Christ' Home," and in it there is a simple picture of the condition of the heart.

He describes our Heart with many rooms. Each one is open to visitors, but we keep one room to ourselves. In the book he imagines giving a tour of his heart to Jesus. He goes through each room and describes the good and not so good parts of the house. He begins with the Study or the Library. He watches the eyes of the Master and feels a bit uncomfortable with the selections on the shelf that filled his mind. They moved on to other rooms. They end up at the hall closet where the Lord exclaims that He smells something dead still remains in there and with a simple transfer of deed, He offered to help clean it up.

What rooms are open to God

This is the moment we can take any racial mistreatment we might have experienced, any deliberate distrust, or anger, or hurt, and give it to God. This is where we can share how much pain we have had from the inequity of being a woman in such a man's world and this is where we can clean out those secrets we have kept which God has known all along and give it away.

We just bow our head and close our eyes and open our mind to Him accepting His love for us.

In What Ways Does God Prove He Cares About Me?

_____

_____

_____

_____

_____

_____

_____

_____

_____

_____

_____

_____

_____

_____

_____

_____

_____

He is Moved by Our Pain

"Jesus wept" — John 11:35

IN THIS DAY of social distancing and in tactile depri-
vation studies have been launched researching the long-
term impact on society from the lack of touch due to the
covid protocols. This feeling of being overwhelmed with
emotion is referred to as "Kama muta" which comes
from the Sanskrit meaning "moved by love". Our emotional codependence on each other is not limited to
physical touch. One researcher shared that the experience of being emotionally moved or touched, although
likely common, has not been subject to significant psy-
chological research, until now.

He goes on to say, Kama Muta is felt when one
observes or engages in events which cause a deepened
sense of oneness with others and motivates devotion to
those relationships. Kama Muta is considered to have
the evolutionary function of facilitating the devotion,

commitment, and connection necessary for human social union. For when Jesus wept, He was connecting. The very act of weeping deepens the connection.

We all have experienced at one time those goose-bumps of a reunion. That intense feeling when hugging. It can be with one person, with a family or team, or with the entire Earth. That is the Kama Muta affect we feel, and Jesus shared that day.

We may think of Jesus as purely business. Healing the sick, feeding the multitudes and casting out devils. Routines of a day in the life of a Messiah. But it was far from the truth. He had friends and formed relationships. Jesus was and is consumed with intimacy with mankind and was emotionally engaged several times, no less than that of His friend Lazarus. He was fully in this human experience. Christ followers are familiar with the miracle of raising from the dead His close friend Lazarus. But what may not have been noticed is what led up to those celebrated events.

Jesus was on the road teaching when word come to Him that His good friend was ill and could die. Jesus' response shook people. They thought He would drop everything and return to His friend's side. But instead, He returns to His teaching and takes a leisurely turn toward His friend.

Four days will pass when He arrives only to be berated by his overwhelmed sister with news that he had already died. Though all along Jesus knew Lazarus would be raised from the dead, yet He was so emotionally touched the Scripture's record, the shortest verse of the Bible. It is found in the gospel account recorded in John 11:35, with the words, "Jesus wept."

God understands tears

Our tears matter. We may feel alone, but we are not alone. More than a moistening system to keep our eye lubricated, we know tears are a form of expression. Emotions are to our heart as what the nervous system is to the body. It indicates something is wrong. We might have trouble knowing what is exactly causing the problem, but we just know it doesn't feel right.

I am such a sap when it comes to tears. I get choked up at every parade when the colors go bye. There isn't a Christmas movie that I don't find special. In fact, I was at a leadership conference in Chicago, when one of the exercises was to name a movie that moved me emotionally and Christmas movies aside my winner was "*Mr. Holland's Opus.*"

It is proposed that emotional tearing, is a unique human behavior, which serves to communicate information to observers to change their behavior. Psychologists see emotional tearing as an invitation to share in the relationship. For instance, emotional tearing could signal appeasement or need for attachment, which in turn fosters social bonding. It is not surprising that tears could communicate emotional information in accordance with the social signals. Thus, we understand that God in the flesh, Jesus, was signaling a call for the people to join Him in His mourning over the city.

Jesus was fully human and fully God at the same time and so He experienced the five human emotions, sadness, joy, anger, hurt, and fear. We may have done our own research on the subject and find much longer lists of emotions, but they are longer because we can keep slicing up the pie into an infinite number of slices but have only one pie. Honestly, they are more hybrids that combine the different lists but I find there are only five true divisions: Sadness, Hurt, Anger, Happiness, and Fear. What is important to understand is we often judge people by their degree of control of their expressions. We can only control the outburst intensity and duration when we understand the core reason for the reaction.

Emotions tell us something is up

Not to make this a psychology book so we will make it simple to understand. Each emotion we experience has a shadow of a core reason that brought upon the response. The expression hits the news, but it is the core feeling that generates the response. Here is the core response for each emotion: Sadness is loss, Happiness is abundance, Anger is respect, Hurt is betrayal and Fear is safety.

The next time one of those emotions are expressed see if it isn't tied to a core feeling. For example, if we get angry when a car cut us off it is because we feel a loss of respect. The other driver made us feel a lower-level value, and we reacted. Consider that we only thought they were a bad driver. But it was deeper. Think how by understanding where the reaction comes from, we can improve all our relationships. If we can honestly identify the core feeling, we are more apt to be able to control our response.

God shares in our grief

Jesus wept after hearing of the fate of Lazarus, though He knew he would bring him back to life, because He sensed loss. Not only of his friend but shared the grief of His sister's loss, Mary, and Martha. He ached over the reality that He may bring his friend back from the dead but knew that one day he will not be there to bring him back later. The intensity of his weeping was also given in the text. This was not a tear trickling down the cheek. The Bible is clear that every part of His body felt the pain.

Chance are we've been at a funeral because of the loss of a co-worker, friend, or family member. There is a void that reassuring words cannot fill. Let's extended this grief toward any event that reminds us we don't have ultimate control of life. A bad diagnosis, job loss, lack of food, housing insecurity etc. All of this can be reflected with the feelings of loss and expressed through sadness.

An expert in psychology explains that emotions are part of the human biology, just so many chemicals helping us regulate our minds and bodies, assisting us to cope with the complexities of making decisions, interacting with people, and finding our way through life. We feel emotions to help us pay attention, focus our attention, and motivate us to action.

We should embrace our feelings as a part of us, helping us to focus and draw attention to something going on. To use the earlier analogy of a driver cutting us off, we can control our feeling by saying to ourselves they don't know me, and I am in no hurry. That isn't a suppressant of our feeling it is embracing the feeling and putting it into the correct category.

When Jesus cried over His friend and at the sight of the city, he was putting His head down to get the job done, He was focusing on its lostness and its redemption.

Don't hold our feelings in

It is a reminder that God places His concern of our heart. Jesus wept because He loves us so much. He loves us as an individual. We may be going through some rough days, but I like an old quote "the most comforting words in the Bible are 'and it came to pass'" Right now it might be hard to take, but it is only temporary. It too shall pass.

In What Ways Does God Prove He Cares About Me?

_____

_____

_____

_____

_____

_____

_____

_____

_____

_____

_____

_____

_____

_____

_____

_____

_____

Feelings of Rejection

"When Martha heard that Jesus was coming, she went out to meet him, but Mary stayed at home. "Lord," Martha said to Jesus, "if you had been here, my brother would not have died." — John 11:20-21 NIV

EVER FEEL REJECTED? Here's a story found in the Bible of a man who did everything right and he still suffered negative consequences. The Gospel of John 9 details the story of a man born blind. All his life he lived in darkness and when he was old enough, he began begging for a living. Until one day he was in the right place at the right time and met Jesus. He was healed by Jesus, a truly miraculous event, right? But the religious leaders of the time were caught up by their own egos.

Hurting?

The religious leaders after interviewing the former blind man and his parents it was from that day on, they were excommunicated from the synagogue for life. The religious leaders were angered by which day of the week the man was healed than the fact they had just witnessed a miraculous event. But the blind man was removed from the synagogue we find the story takes a very personal turn. As the gospel records:

> *"Jesus heard that they had thrown him out, and when he found him, he said, "Do you believe in the Son of Man?"* — John 9:35 NIV

Mirroring the story of the lost sheep, where the good shepherd leaves the 99 sheep to find the one who wandered off, a picture everyone in Jesus' day would have knowledge of, Jesus heard that the man was barred from the synagogue and with His concern for the well-being of the man, Jesus sought him out. As we see He finds him and reaffirms his faith.

Jesus shared with him His divine Presence and continued His explanation of a personal God who rescues. Disappointment fills our lives. Certainly, my job loss was not part of the plan I had for my life or that of Julie. I expected to go on and on for at least a couple of years more. But God had another plan that He had not let me in on. My wife took the high road and tried to get me to understand that I didn't count the saving nature of our Lord. Perhaps He spared me of some heartache I didn't see on this current trajectory.

While the words Julie offered shared some comfort, I still looked for answers. I found it in the repeated examples in the Bible. It is full of stories like us, and now we have the benefit of decades to see how what appeared to be tragedy at the time, turned into a victory. God does know what He's doing we just need to have the patience and wait to see how our own personal season cliffhanger turns out. There is some reassurance today to know that God is on our side. Do we need a bolder statement?

> *"Do not take revenge, my dear friends, but*
> *leave room for God's wrath, for it is written:*
> *"It is mine to avenge; I will repay," says the*
> *Lord."* — Romans 12:19 NIV

Life is unfair

Someone wisely once said that we can do something completely right but still end up with negative circumstances. Life is frequently not fair. We may be the focus of the inequity of this world and find ourselves fighting for our life. We can become bitter and let it blind our soul and color our future. Or we can have confidence that God will balance the scales.

The word Karma is thrown around in a manner that gives us solace that we will get vindicated at some time. We may even quote the "eye for an eye" or the reaping and sowing verses of the Bible that makes us feel some sort of revenge. But what do we do when Paul writes, not to seek revenge? Because it is an endless cycle of pain. When God intervenes, it will be at the right time and place. Consider the revelation the Old Testament man Joseph had.

Since his youth his older brothers were jealous of him and the adoration or favoritism that he received from their father was deafening. Finally, they were going to kill him and blame it on a wild animal. But cooler heads prevailed and they through him into a well and eventually he is sold to slave traders traveling by and then in service to the Pharoah himself. His epic quote comes when he is reunited with his brothers years later and they know Joseph is now in a place that could bring about their death.

False security

The brothers assumed that as long as their father was still alive, they thought they were safe. However, Jacob was old and ailing and finally he died. The brothers in fear of their lives now years later stand before their brother and here was Joseph's surprising response,

"You intended to harm me, but God intended it for good to accomplish what is now being done, the saving of many lives."
— *Genesis 50:20 NIV*

He was letting them know, looking back he could see God's hand all over the good and bad times. It was tough but God had a much bigger plan they did. So, we're there wondering how can God use his circumstance? I don't know the end game, but there is plan for us if we just don't fight it. This the reason I am not a fan of people saying something is successful or not. What appears to be one way could turn completely around. Let God be the judge and leave it to Him.

Holocaust lesson

Corrie Ten Boom, lived through the holocaust, how could anything good come from this? She lost both her parents and her sister Betsy in the concentrations camps as they tried to hide targeted Jews in their home. She makes a remarkable statement, that essentially that this is what the past is for. That every experience God gives us, and every person He puts in our lives is the perfect preparation for the future that only He can see.

We see only what is today. God sees eternal.

In What Ways Does God Prove He Cares About Me?

_____

_____

_____

_____

_____

_____

_____

_____

_____

_____

_____

_____

_____

_____

_____

_____

Darkness surrounds

"Neither is there salvation in any other: for there is none other name under heaven given among men, whereby we must be saved." — Acts 4:12 NIV

SPARTA, WISCONSIN IS known by many bike lovers for its conversion of old railway lines into bike trails. Although I am not one of those tight pants avid bike jockeys, for fun I had asked my wife about taking a weekend and spending it riding the trails. She consented and within a few days we traveled to the woods. One of the highlights was to traverse through a tunnel about one mile long. Julie said she was taking a pass on this part of the journey at the mouth of the dark tunnel, but she would gladly wait for me to ride to the other end and back if I wanted to go. So, I launched off.

Darkness surrounds me

In a short time, I was surrounded by darkness. I stopped at one point just out of curiosity and I had trouble seeing my hand in front of my face. But when I looked up, I could see the proverbial light at the end of the tunnel. I reasoned that if I aimed my bike in the middle of the light, I would be okay. That is until my bike hit the side of the tunnel not realizing I had veered off course. I tried to go a little closer toward the light and once again I hit the wall. At that point I realized the darkness was so great I was unable to navigate my way to the end. So, I turned around and headed back toward the start of my journey and Julie.

Sometimes we can have a dark period come into our life that makes it hard to navigate. Part of us knows there's an end to the tunnel up ahead but the darkness can be overwhelming. Just knowing that the light is coming is not enough. If I had a flashlight, things might have been better, if I was riding with a friend or guide who knew the way I would have made it to the other side. This is the beauty and value of spending time finding Jesus in every dark moment. He is like a guide that has been there before and knows the way. His strength is our confidence. I know what it feels to be in the dark, both physically and spiritually. I know how hard it is to keep pedaling not knowing if we're headed in the right direction. I found great comfort in relying on the writings of others, who stayed the course. I flooded my time with inspirational devotionals. Instead of feeling sorry for myself, I took to reading the Psalms, one at a time avoiding the trap of making it a job.

Jesus had made fast progress to this point with His ragtag group of followers. By the time we get to the Gospel John chapter 14, Jesus had lived, eaten, drank together with the disciples for nearly three years. What's more Philip had heard Jesus teach and seen Him do wonderous miracles. So, imagine the disappointment Jesus must have felt when those closest to Him still didn't know who He was. Philip declared what was probably on the minds of the disciples when he said,

> *"…Lord, show us the Father and that will be enough for us. Jesus answered: "Don't you know me, Philip, even after I have been among you such a long time? Anyone who has seen me has seen the Father. How can you say, 'Show us the Father'?"* — John 14:8-9

Following the status quo

If you have ever ventured out on a trip you understand there is always the possibility of unplanned events interrupting the best of intentions. Such was one occasion that I had when skiing with a group of friends. We had been out for most of the day, and I had taken a lot of good-natured kidding about being one of the most careful members of the group. Until one day when the lead person of our pack decided to do some, what was known as tree bashing. This is when skiers go off the groomed trail and head into the powdered snow in the tree lines.

They suddenly they took a left turn and exited the ski trail. That was reckless, but I didn't want to seem a prude and if I just stayed on the tracks of the others ahead of me, I reasoned it was safe. Think of the logic of that decision, if I went in the path of those of everybody else before me, I would be okay. Never thinking that person may have died, and I had just never arrived at their lifeless body yet.

So, I took a hard left and kept my two skis in the grooves of the skis set before me. It was daring and fun racing among the trees smashing against low hanging branches. That is until the trail suddenly turned left, along with my trusty grooves again. It was too fast, and I couldn't make the turn. I reasoned again that I will just continue my present course until I would come out on the other side.

Flawed logic

The only problem with this already flawed thinking was quite to my surprise when the trail ended, and I was six feet above the ground with nothing but air. And since I don't have wings and gravity was still a natural force I came crashing down. Landing on my chest it where it successfully forced the air out of my lungs.

Trying not to appear weak I simply worked to regain my breath as my friends were laughing and circling round me. The funny thing was they admired my effort at flying like the Wright brothers of airplane fame, while I was hoping they would not notice my crash. All because I didn't find the way through the woods.

That was the challenge the disciples had faced. They felt safe if it conformed to their line of thinking, like grooves in the snow by ski's. But Jesus wanted more, he had hoped that the time they had spent together would be clearer at this point. Jesus could never be accused of being one that played it safe and expected, but when He did deviate from the trail it was not to boost His ego or get an adrenalin rush, but to glorify the Father. While Philip thought he was a star pupil, he failed the class. Jesus' reaction tells it all. His words speak volume about the depth of a relationship He wanted more with His earthly disciples.

More personal He couldn't have been. They been together and experienced many things. There were times when they were with Jesus just watching Him and at other times they were paired up and sent on their own with a great deal of success. When Philip asked for Jesus to show him the Father, despite all the power being displayed through their ministry, Jesus knew they still didn't get it. This question by Philip acted like a spiritual thermometer, it revealed how well they fully understood. It showed they failed to connect.

This is a reminder that we can be raised in church and still not feel the closeness of God. Going each week and having perfect attendance should not be our goal. To feel His touch or know His grace, that is life! In other words, I don't know your spiritual condition and far it from me that I would set myself up as a judge, but it is more than going through motions. Discipleship is more than writing a personal check. Discipleship is more than serving on a committee at church or serving in a position of authority. We can be very full of ourself but be far from God. Jesus addresses this when He shares the story of a religious man and a poor man:

> *"But the tax collector stood at a distance. He would not even look up to heaven, but beat his breast and said, 'God, have mercy on me, a sinner.' I tell you that this man, rather than the other, went home justified before God. For all those who exalt themselves will be humbled, and those who humble themselves will be exalted."* — Luke 18:13-14 NIV

Break through

I have traveled much around the nation. Usually by plane to the various cities. I am still in wonder and awe when the passenger plane takes off and breaks through the clouds on a grey overcast day, there is the bright sun waiting for us. But just as a cloudy sky hides the sun, it doesn't mean the sun is not there. Oh, it is as bright as ever. He waits for us to reach out and embrace Him.

We all need to take the time in the darkest moments to keep on pedaling toward the light. This is our moment to choose how we will spend the time.

In What Ways Does God Prove He Cares About Me?

Believing Without Seeing

"By faith we understand that the universe was formed at God's command, so that what is seen was not made out of what was visible." — Hebrews 11:3 NIV

THERE ARE SOME that push faith as the ultimate prize to find. There are so called faith teachers and faith preachers. Some churches are so wrapped up in the acquisition of faith they choose to name their building including the word "faith." What do we do when we're feeling a little low on faith? This could be just one of those moments. We are down in the dumps, maybe even feeling a bit embarrassed. I want us to remember how many Bible stories remind us of God doing the miraculous when there is no faith present at all. Instead, we find a lesson about God's love or sovereignty.

Faith is not as important

One of the most famous goof ups of the disciples was when they were aboard a ship that was in the middle of a stormy sea. Jesus was exhausted from teaching and healing so many people, so he slept in the rear of the boat. This was significant as that part of the boat would be most easily swept over by the waves in a stormy sea. Jesus wasn't worried. But his faithful disciples feared for their lives. I am sure as fishermen they had encountered storms before. But this time instead of relying on their own skills or faith, they wake up Jesus and ask for His help. He awakens and calms the sea with a command. No faith, but dependence. On one hand they were a disappointment, on the other hand they knew who to turn too. That is our choice also.

We learn from their disappointing moments as well as their victories. A few days after the resurrection and Thomas was not present at the first appearance of Jesus, he had only heard the rumors. Naturally, he questioned the word of the women. He listened to the stories from the women who were at the tomb. He hears the excitement in their voices of the disciples describing their encounter with the risen Christ, but his objective brain could not accept the words of others. Then he throws down a gauntlet of sorts. The only way that he will believe is through a personal experience.

"But he said to them, "Unless I see the nail marks in his hands and put my finger where the nails were, and put my hand into his side, I will not believe." — John 20:25 NIV

He was clear if not specific. At first glance we might be critical of his statement. "Why doesn't he accept the testimony of others?" we say. But I for one am excited that he wanted hard core proof. He refused to be caught up in hopeful hysteria. He wanted to touch Jesus for himself. Longing for a personal encounter, he would have to wait a week. Then suddenly:

"Then he said to Thomas, 'Put your finger here; see my hands. Reach out your hand and put it into my side. Stop doubting and believe.'" — John 20:27

Jesus welcomed the personal challenge. If that is was what it took to firm up their faith, He wanted to be touched and His declaration for future Christ followers.

"Then Jesus told him, "Because you have seen me, you have believed; blessed are those who have not seen and yet have believed." — John 20:29 NIV

I can still feel the tug

We are a part of the generation who believe though we cannot see. Even without touching, we can imagine feeling God's Presence near us. We can reach out and touch Him today. I am forever impressed with a story Evangelist Billy Graham once told. He described a day about a child at a beach holding on to what appeared to be a string attached to a kite. But the kite was so high it disappeared into the clouds and could not be seen by the young boy any longer yet held on. Until a man came up to him and questioned the lad about what he was doing. Here he was holding on to what seemed like an empty string. The man asked, How do you know it's still there? To which the boy replied, Because I can still feel it's tug.

We may be waiting for a miracle, but God doesn't work that way. We ask for a sign or bargain with God by pledging our devotion. The truth is we came to a point when we just must believe. We see any answer we get to our request will be just like that empty string. High it goes into the sky but it's rise can be enough, we are at the crossroads, we can be like Thomas who wants to see more, or we can be the boy who just feels the tug. One will always expect a sign but the other will look for a meaningful relationship.

Is love real?

We forget that the most powerful things in this world are not tangible. We see them so often we forget that we live with the intangible all the time. For example, I often use a photocopy machine, but I have no clue how it works, and yet I have no doubt it will work. Or consider the love a boyfriend has for his girlfriend. We would be hard pressed to convince him that love, isn't real. But wait a minute, we can't measure it according to scientific standards in a laboratory. We can't touch it or see it. How about the hate we see it on the streets during protests over a certain belief? The hate can be destructive, and the belief could even be wrong, and may even be misguided. We might not be able to convince them to change their point of view. These examples may be real, so why can't faith be real? There is one verse from the Bible that sums it up when it states,

> *"Now faith is confidence in what we hope for and assurance about what we do not see."* — Hebrews 11:1 NIV

It started right up

We use faith all the time. When I went to my car this morning and I pressed the button to start it, I gave no thought that it would not start. I had no proof it would not start, it operated the night before, but I had no physical proof it would start or not start. I just accepted its reliability. I heard one person boldly saying that to believe in evolution took more faith than to believe in creation. That might sound bizarre but think of it. Which is a firmer belief? Through evolution which has only conceptual proof that the odds of some of the most complex creatures just came together out of random selection within the goo, not just once but multiple times or that a Divine Creator intentionally with and great care put things together? Which takes more faith?

That is our choice. We might not know why certain things work we just know they do as some architect or engineer designed it. Yet we can't escape the kite string. In our heart of hearts, we feel a tug, so we know He's there. If we let Him in everything around, will make sense. Until we let Him in, we will be full of questions. Not that we will know the wisdom of the universe, we just will not care as much because He is managing it.

In What Ways Does God Prove He Cares About Me?

A Rough Childhood

*"When I was a child, I talked like a child,
I thought like a child, I reasoned like
a child. When I became a man, I put
the ways of childhood behind me."* —
I Corinthians 13:11 NIV

WE LIVE IN a very youthful society. For the first time in human history, youth have become a model of emulation by the older population, rather than the wise aged leading youth. It doesn't take long to notice the impact. Boomers dress like youth, listen to youthful music and even embrace forms of technology that have been used principally used by youth.

It is a curious thing in that we have the greatest lopsided world than found in human history records. We hear of the greying of America but while it is true the growth is among the elderly like never that it is confined to the demographic of the United States. When we look on a global scale, there are more youth in India than America the United Kingdom combined. Certainly, we are already living in an age of youth dominance.

Spoiled our first child

We had our first child after three years of marriage and couldn't wait until her first Christmas. Lori was born in the early days of August so she would be all starry eyed for her first holiday. We wanted it all for that first year, so we made sure we terrified her with the Santa at the shopping mall, bought her an ornament with her name on it and bought her lots of gifts to insure lots of pictures. This is a common reaction by first time parents. We want to see our child be overwhelmed at the holiday. We were successful.

Jesus always had a special relationship with children. Their innocence and faith are unmatched. There is no more precious mental picture than that of children rushing forward to touch Jesus. And we can see him bending down to them and lifting them up one or two kids in his arms. Children are not jaded by the world and that naivete is both good and bad. They are open to possibilities of the future but can be vulnerable to the wickedness of this world.

Jesus recognized that kids are the future and even stands by their side in bad times when he warns the price tag for mistreatment. He says,

*"If anyone causes one of these little ones—
those who believe in me—to stumble, it
would be better for them to have a large
millstone hung around their neck and to
be drowned in the depths of the sea." —*
Matthew18:6 NIV

No Bible story carries a better example of children
being used by God than that found in the story of the
boyhood of the prophet Samuel. We picture him as an
old man that terrified the residents with his truth giving
when he would visit to a village. But there is a prequel
for his future telling life which is found in I Samuel
1-3. He himself was literally an answer to a desperate
mother's plea. We learn that the childless woman who
appeared to bystanders as though her cries were that of
a drunk woman by her desperation in prayer. She ultimately promised that if the Lord gave her a child, she
would surrender him to full time service to God. I love
this Bible verse that God said, "He remembered." God
cared so much because she was the one who had such
passion with her prayer. She wept and groaned; God did
not ignore her. And she fulfill her promise to set aside
her first born son for God's service. She maintained
contact with him each year by making him clothes and
delivering them.

A rough childhood

He was only a boy that was being raised by a scoundrel high priest, and his immoral sons. It was surrounded by inequity as a child that he first heard the voice of God. The Bible even goes as far to say that the Word of God was "rare in those days." He had no example, no model that could develop his spiritual life, he was just a child. All he knew was he just heard a voice.

> *"The lamp of God had not yet gone out, and Samuel was lying down in the house of the Lord, where the ark of God was. Then the Lord called Samuel. Samuel answered, 'Here I am.' And he ran to Eli and said, 'Here I am you called me.' But Eli said, 'I did not call; go back and lie down.' So, he went and lay down."*

> *"Again, the Lord called, 'Samuel!' And Samuel got up and went to Eli and said, 'Here I am you called me.' 'My son,' Eli said, 'I did not call; go back and lie down.' Now Samuel did not yet know the Lord: The word of the Lord had not yet been revealed to him."* — I Samuel 3:3-10 NIV

Three times he hears a voice in the darkness calling him and three times Eli thought he was dreaming in his sleep. Then it dawned on the high priest Eli that God might be speaking to the boy and encouraged the young Samuel that the next time he hears the voice just remain in his bed and make yourself available to God by responding to the voice. God did indeed call once more, and he answered in all his childlikeness. Then God revealed the future to him.

Jesus really expanded the role of children in the kingdom of God by saying it isn't "children" per se, it is a child-like attitude we should cultivate. In a spiritual sense we can get in our own way. We over think God's interaction with us much like the dumb blind sidedness of Eli the high priest. We can take a few times to finally see God's hand in all of this. When God is speaking to us, it's our choice to ignore Him or misunderstand Him. I think it is safe to say, we get it wrong more often than we get it right, but it sharpens our spiritual skills bringing us closer to God in the meantime.

It is worth the trying. Instead of being quick to get out of bed and look for an earthly answer to our dilemma maybe we should lie there and let God know we're open to His plan. This is to acknowledge the sovereignty of God. As difficult as our situation might be He has a way out of the forest of trouble we find ourself. But we must slow down long enough to see it.

I had the children rushing up to me experience once in my life when I was visiting Mexico, and it is almost over whelming. I was exiting my airplane and we passengers were swarmed with children selling trinkets and paper flowers. The desperateness of their poverty was obvious. It was later that I learned their parents had ordered their children to sell to the tourists and in some situations, they were beaten if they had a poor sales showing.

Imagine the time of Jesus when as the children lunged forward past the disciples, they only saw inconvenience and trouble. Jesus saw this as an opportunity to teach those who followed Him. There were no trinkets or paper flowers among the handmade crafts they had that day. The children were without abandoned and wanted to be by Jesus. And Jesus recognized the innocence in their eyes and sweeps them up in His arms scolding His disciples. This is a lesson for all of us.

> *"People were also bringing babies to Jesus for him to place his hands on them. When the disciples saw this, they rebuked them. But Jesus called the children to him and said, "Let the little children come to me, and do not hinder them, for the kingdom of God belongs to such as these. Truly I tell you, anyone who will not receive the kingdom*

of God like a little child will never enter it."
— Luke 18:15-17 NIV

Begging us to come

It is a sign of our attitude toward God, not of pride but to come to God humbly and without reservation. It's an innocence of trust that will not be turned away. It's a knowledge that we can always come to Him. Today, He is down on one knee bidding for us to come. Picture yourself like a child running up to Jesus. Just us and Him in a warm embrace. Maybe we are giggling. Maybe we're just need to cry a little. It's okay, He wants us to come to Him even when we are broken. Especially when we are broken.

Watching Tik Tok?

How important is a child? In Jesus day, children were treated more like a commodity in a largely agrarian society, than a cute tiny tot. The children had chores each day, that would cause American children to squirm. They would work in the fields from the early morning until past sunset, not sit at home watching Tik Tok or television. We have a life of comfort and ease in comparison.

Can we race up to Jesus now and feel His acceptance? Stop thinking about the wrongs we have done and know He will accept us as we are. We're just an innocent little child in His eyes getting a second chance. Consider that Isaiah in giving his prophetic statement of the future he is describing how things will be run.

> *"The wolf also shall dwell with the lamb, and the leopard shall lie down with the kid; and the calf and the young lion and the fatling together; and a little child shall lead them."* — Isaiah 11:6 NIV

Someday the world will be a land of peace. What was once an enemy will be a companion. The world as we know it will be restored to the way it was supposed to be as God intended. Children will be leading around former wild beasts. The lesson here is not just for the future. Note how Jesus doesn't just show kindness, He takes the occasion to reference the child like nature we should have. There is unquestioning trust. There is no hesitation by the kids. They knew instinctively Jesus would allow their rush to greet Him, and welcome it. There was no hesitation on their part.

Imagine how different the world would be if a fireman hesitated to help, people, and save property. Much would be lost if while we wait for action to be taken committees were forming. What if a policeman didn't immediately act? Lives could be lost. It is often said that first responders run toward the danger while others run from the danger. During trouble, we must have a plan already in place so we can respond quickly.

Trust

Consider the traits of a child to which Jesus referred. A child first intuitively trusts their parents, it is hardwired in them from birth. No one taught them in school. They put their belief in parents that they will be cared for as a priority. If we watch the "news" it is replete with stories of people gone wrong. So there are exceptions, but they are exceptions, and most kids do trust their parents.

Part of that trust is depending on our provision. From their earliest days they count on their parents to feed them. That turns into clothing. They can't speak for themselves or dress themselves or cook for themselves, they simple express themselves and we come running. We are well trained.

How about God, he considers us to be one of His children. He calls us sons and daughters not disciples like pupils. Or slaves like He is the master. He sees us in entirely different way. The references to us are familial. Children with God as the Father.

Proud mother

The second trait that child exhibits that is treasured by God is that of potential. He believes in us more than an earthly father does for their kid. It was my final year of college and the weekend before graduation. The college was hosting a reception and my mother, and I were mingling among the students and a few teachers when suddenly I came face to face with the President of our school. He was very well versed in talking to the parents of students when he made a very general comment about my abilities as being impressive. To which my mother responded that she had no doubt I would stand out, in true mother fashion. I was embarrassed by her bravado, but the President was very gracious.

Yes, God believes in our potential. He believes in us. "Babies and toddlers are keen observers of their world, actively and accurately interpreting what people and objects do and why they do it—like little scientists. Preschoolers use words to investigate their world. One study found that preschoolers can ask 75 questions per hour, not as bids for attention but to "extract" information from the adults around them. We might find it annoying and at times embarrassing. But they are eager to learn and know no timetable other than now. One time I remember the scandal that was created in a kid class when my daughter announced to the class that I walked around the house naked. The teacher inquired of me for some clarification, and I explained that on some occasions I had worn only boxer shorts at night. To her being out of clothes meant I was naked and, in her innocence, told others. Without a life bias their potential is unrestricted by their past experiences or education.

Innocence

Finally, the last trait we want to highlight is that of innocence. Children embrace life thinking everything is going to go their way. Often life does make a path for a child or adult with confidence. Even if the record shows otherwise, their experience is limited to only their creativity. As adults we try very hard not to fail. As a result, we are more circumspect when it comes to our ideas. We will self-elect to not try something because we have learned the concepts of embarrassment and failure. A child enjoys a certain naivete when it comes to stretching for new possibilities. And their bold actions actually the yield of possible success.

Jesus could see that in the eyes of the children that just spontaneously ran up to him. It honestly never occurred to them they might be put aside. Us adults might have wrestled with so many issues that we reasoned would be a barrier which might keep us from turning back to God. While we are standing there in the crowd thinking about all the reasons why God wouldn't want us to trouble Him, kids will run past us to Jesus' waiting arms.

We do that today in a symbolic way. We can list in our imagination all the reasons why our feelings or needs are unimportant to God. Afterall, He is occupied with management of the universe or what we consider are the "legitimate" needs of others. While it might seem rather obvious to say, God is able to multi-task. I know multi-tasking is more of a current term, but it covers it quite nicely. God can do more than one thing at a time once. It's kind of like our bodies. It can do multiple tasks at the same time. We take a breath and eat, and our blood continues to move through our veins all at the same time. And the feeling that our needs are not important or considered legitimate are just wrong. God does care and wants us to reach out to Him past our self-doubt.

In What Ways Does God Prove He Cares About Me?

_____

_____

_____

_____

_____

_____

_____

_____

_____

_____

_____

_____

_____

_____

_____

94 Million Searches

"For God so loved the world that he gave his one and only Son, that whoever believes in him shall not perish but have eternal life."
— John 3:16 NIV

WE'VE SEEN IT painted across the bellies of fans at football games, we've seen it on posters and in the end zones. The television camera always seemed to capture the "Bible verse guy" that was talking about the love of God. I hadn't noticed him lately and wanted to know more of the backstory. The sign fold-open poster read simply, "John 3:16." Nothing more, nothing less and with each display in the end zone lots of folks went online to see what he was talking about. If you're not familiar with the quote from the Bible, it reads:

"For God so loved the world, that he gave his only begotten Son, that whosoever believeth

> *in him should not perish, but have ever-*
> *lasting life."* — John 3:16 KJV

As it turned out the end zone poster routine was made famous by a man named Rollen Stewart. He appeared at multiple sporting events in the United States and around the world. It is said that he was never paid for his publicity, but various Christians would donate their tickets so he could be in just the right spot.

However, the most famous display of John 3:16 didn't come from Rollen Stewart, it was made by the football player, Tim Tebow, when he played for the Florida Gators. According to Mr. Tebow's own testimony, in the late 2000's it was popular to smear some black eyeshadow right below their eyes to reduce reflection, but others made it away to communicate to the fans. Some wrote their mom's name or their area code among other things. But Tim Tebow being a devout Christian chose to carry the Bible message "Phil" under one eye and "4:3" under the other eye," which meant to stand for the abbreviation of the Bible passage, Philippians 4:3, which reads,

> *"I can do all this through him who gives me*
> *strength."* — NIV

It was a nice uplifting verse from the Bible to encourage the performance of all his teammates at a game. He wore it until their last game, when he felt he should change the verse from Phil 4:3 to John 3:16, because it summed up what Christianity was all about. After getting the clearance from his parents and coach he changed the passage to John 3:16 for his next game which was the 2009 SEC college football game.

94 million searches

The remarkable results were discovered after the game. He was out to dinner with the coach, when the coach gets a phone call from the team's PR guy. They just found out that over 94 million people had googled a request of the meaning of John 3:16. Was that the reason God moved on Tim's heart? Did God use Tim to touch 94 million souls with the message of God's love? Only eternity will reveal the stories.

But wait there's more. Tim kept up the practice of wearing John 3:16 under his eyes even into the professional football league after college. According to Mr. Tebow, three years later to the day they were playing the Pittsburgh Steelers in Denver. He was playing for the Broncos at year, they won their play-off game. There was a press conference scheduled and right before the team's media blitz was to start, the PR person for the team stopped Tim to tell him about the game. He told him it was incredible but Tim, "you threw for 316 yards, you averaged 31.6 yards per throw, your yards per rush were 3.16 yards, the ratings for the night were 31.6, and the time of possession was 31.06 minutes. Over and over came the confirmation to wear John 3:16. Mr. Tebow didn't know it at the time, but God was keeping the stats all along. That means Tim may have gotten stopped in his rush so that his number would be exactly 316 yards. He may have felt like he failed to go further, but the numbers were right.

With God nothing is random, He is involved with the outcomes. He cares about us right now and He can position us for a win, it might be different then what we hoped or thought, but trust what He's doing. John 3:16 sums up the value of Christianity like nothing else. It is a love story. In it He carries the heart of God for us. It is a reminder of the reason God came and the incredible price He paid to be with us.

That very special sacrificial love is often translated from one of the Greek words for love, "Agape," in the New Testament. The word he chose not only this describes His relationship with us, but how we should treat others. The religious leaders in Jesus' time routinely followed Him around. One day a leader try to trap Jesus, asked, which commandment is most important? Jesus answered:

> *"Answered Jesus, 'is this: 'Hear, O Israel: The Lord our God, the Lord is one. Love the Lord your God with all your heart and*

> *with all your soul and with all your mind*
> *and with all your strength.' The second is*
> *this: Love your neighbor as yourself. There*
> *is no commandment greater than these.'"*
> — Mark 12:29-31 NIV

In other words, they are two sides of the same coin. He treated us with love and expects our treatment of others to be with the same standard. And with that He set the standard for everything else. If we let love be our standard by which we measure all our deals whether with God or man, we can't go wrong.

Fall in love, wrong

He transforms our view of love. We no longer "fall" in love like it just happened to us, as is commonly portrayed in our culture. Love now becomes a choice. We serve others as a premeditated decision setting aside our preferences in virtue of the needs of others. It is critical we understand that distinction. Take for example the three words used in the New Testament. Philo, Eros and Agape. Each one was treated differently in the translation but can be found clearer in the context they are used.

Consider, "Philo" it is meant as a love relationship but only as that of friend. That is how Philadelphia got its modern name. Then take "Eros" from which in today's English we get, "Erotic" as we can imagine it is reference to sexual expression of love. And then the last Greek word in the New Testament that was translated love is "agape," and it means to the point of sacrifice.

If you are still having trouble keeping the words straight think about their use in the real world. I love my children, But I love my wife and love my car differently than others. Thus, I express myself differently in each circumstance. God wants us to see people in various ways. We have an obligation to our wife that is different to our kids and car. While my car may need an oil change every three months, I don't think telling my wife or showing her affection once every three months will be enough.

As important as John 3;16 is to Christianity I think it is incomplete without reading the emotion in the following verse in John 3:17, that is rarely quoted. It reads:

> *"For God did not send his Son into the world*
> *to condemn the world, but to save the world*
> *through him."* — John 3:17 NIV

For those of who lived in fear of God era the following verse of Scripture lends us some peace. God didn't send Jesus to be a faultfinder. Goodness knows we don't need any help with that and all the guilt that comes with that. He wasn't a finger pointer on purpose, He came for one purpose and one purpose only, to die and redeem us, and through that death on the cross convey a clearer image of God is like. Can we find fault in ourself? Of course, all of us can write a list of things that to us would be unlovely or maybe even embarrassing.

Honest evaluation

The way we find our way back to God is to start with some honest evaluation of our life. We're sitting there thinking about our life. And if we're honest we will find areas of improvement. In the past we might have just said, nobody's perfect. However, Jesus gave His life on the cross so we could be released from the endless chain of sin and finally be free.

Putting others to the head of the line is not natural to us. We tend to make decisions that are profitable to us, financially or relationally. We don't want people to think less of us. Jesus is asking us to reconsider. We are still looking for Him to be on the mountaintop or in a church building when he is down the street at the hospital or in the jail cell giving hope.

Jesus visits Washington

In the seventies I came across an interesting article that applies to us still today. It was as if Jesus came on a plane to visit Washington D.C. In the fictious story we find Jesus exiting from His plane, going down the stair case and meeting a delegation of dignitaries on the tarmac. A scuffle soon breaks out over who gets to ride in the lead car with Jesus and in the middle of the debate, Jesus is nowhere to be found.

The story goes on to relate that a nationwide man-hunt is begun, to search for the presence of Jesus. They immediately assumed He was at the capital, but no results. Then the search parties looked among the grounds and building of the White House, still nothing. They even spoke to people at the congress, but they came up empty handed and finally they expanded the search. And in the early hours of the morning the following day they found Him at a soup kitchen helping.

This is a fictional tale, but it illustrates what lengths Jesus is willing to go to demonstrate His love for us. He cares about humanity. Not politics. Even though both sides of the aisle and every media outlet representing politicians seem to feel they have a monopoly on His attention and their agenda.

Do we have a favorite Bible verse? Maybe John 3:16 works for us? Or maybe there is a different verse we might consider to be our favorite. According to one app. which tracks Bible searches we might be surprised what the worldwide search discovered. The hands down favorite in the world is Joshua 1:9. This verse was the most highlighted, bookmarked, and shared in the app in 2017. The creators of the app. revealed that they shared the results based on the 297,811,840 installations of the app in 2017. It reads:

> *"This is my command—be strong and coura-*
> *geous! Do not be afraid or discouraged. For*
> *the Lord, your God is with you wherever*
> *you go." —Joshua 1:9 NIV*

Once again, He demonstrates His love with these words. They are meant to encourage us and build our confidence. Most importantly is that He will "go" with us. He isn't just sitting on the sidelines rooting us on. That is nice, but how much more important knowing He is right there. He has joined our race.

In What Ways Does God Prove He Cares About Me?

_____

_____

_____

_____

_____

_____

_____

_____

_____

_____

_____

_____

_____

_____

_____

_____

_____

A Nation Off Course

"if my people, who are called by my name,
will humble themselves and pray and seek
my face and turn from their wicked ways,
then I will hear from heaven, and I will
forgive their sin and will heal their land."
— II Chronicles 7:14 NIV

DO WE NEED stats to illustrate our need of God as a nation? Just watch the evening news. Shootings, deaths, plagues, poverty, hunger, the list goes on and on as man tries to sort out the issues of our time. It's been said the news never changes from day to day just the names who it affects. This not a call for what some might say are "the good old days," What are the "good ole days," we say? It is typically a call back to the age of prosperity in the fifties.

People who use that phrase forgot about the World Wars and the lives lost to make that prosperity possible.

It was not without cost. But isn't there always a cost involved to see prosperity and peace? It is more simply a call to status quo. The affluent and people in charge use this to maintain control and hold on to a remembrance of past ideals. Usually, an inaccurate belief of the past, void of the hard times and elevating the times of abundance.

We tend to romanticize the past and but it was hard back then too. People still mistreated one another while trying to control others with the power structure of the time. Justice was still in the eyes of the rich and powerful. It is appropriate to start this chapter with the conclusion of the previous chapter, the fictional story of Jesus visiting our capital. Jesus had ministered in private and in public for around three years.

Ministry winding down

In Luke 19:41, we find Jesus' life and ministry winding down. His popularity among the masses has been rising as He fed the poor and healed the sick while giving hope to the zealots who wanted to see Roman rule to end through a violent insurrection. But all the dreams of others were to come to a close as Jesus took a decidedly did a hard turn. He is facing an unwanted crescendo and is about to enter Jerusalem for the last time. He climbs a ridge that overlooks the city and pauses. I am sure his disciples became nervous as they did every time Jesus did something unplanned.

The disciples didn't like the large gathered crowds. They bristled when spontaneously children rushed up to meet Jesus. And they certainly didn't like it when He turned to his followers and said "we can't send these people away without feeding this more than five thousand people with our provisions," but again, He does something unprecedented. That's what love does, spontaneous acts. He climbs down from his mule and walks a short distance.

> *"As he approached Jerusalem and saw the city, he wept over it"* — Luke 19:41 NIV

The people of Jerusalem were excited. They thought this was the beginning of a good time. Jesus would be king, and the Romans would no longer rule over them. However, they didn't understand the nature of that day. Cheering fans even lined the parade route and threw down to the ground freshly cut palm branches and then grabbed their very garments to provide a pavement like a king. To the people it was an exciting day.

But Jesus understood the gravity and personal nature of what was about to happen. He was about to redeem the souls of each man and woman and child on the planet. Individually completely once and for all. And for Him the intensity of the moment was not celebration, but sad ignorance of the waving people. Not since the tomb of Lazarus or will in the Garden of Gethsemane has Jesus wept.

People would watch Him, and some might even have thought He is going to enter the crowd as He climbs down from the mule, but instead he kneels and cries at the crushing burden that is His alone to bear. The sin of the world.

If there is any doubt in our heart that He cares about us, let it be silenced. His care for us brought Jesus to His knees. He loves us and for that reason alone He continued His journey into Jerusalem and facing the future cross.

In What Ways Does God Prove He Cares About Me?

_____

_____

_____

_____

_____

_____

_____

_____

_____

_____

_____

_____

_____

_____

_____

_____

_____

_____

Love vs. Law

*"Teacher, which is the greatest command-
ment in the Law?" Jesus replied: "'Love
the Lord your God with all your heart and
with all your soul and with all your mind.'
This is the first and greatest commandment."*
— Matthew 22:36-40 NIV

IT WAS A Sunday afternoon and normally we are nap
takers at that time. I had given Julie my quick kiss to
lay down for an hour, but something interrupted my
rest. I thought to myself how many times the words
"law" and "love" are found in the Bible. Well, the nap
time was gone because I had to know. It is a surprising
study to search for those two words. It wasn't a scientific study, but I was just curious. And according to one
online Bible the word for "Love" is found no less than
425 times.

It was found it was nearly twice as often as the New Testament.. The Old Testament with its battles and plagues still talks about "love" more often than New Testament. And when it came to the word for "law," there was another surprise! "Love" was found more often than "Law" in the Old Testament. The same place that tells us about the destruction of the cities of Sodom and Gomorrah, that gave us the Ten Commandments, and told about Noah's flood, talked about law less than love. Where did we get such a distorted view of God? Oh, how He loves us!

God of love

We picture a God of rules and thunder, when in truth He is reaching out. No doubt the "law" is important but let's not forget the "law" can be a way to protect us. We can look at the Law as a fence keeping us inside or as a barrier to keep predators out. Jesus had a view about the Law that the Jews of His time wrapped themselves piously into:

> *"Teacher, which is the greatest command-ment in the Law?" Jesus replied: "'Love the Lord your God with all your heart and with all your soul and with all your mind.' This is the first and greatest commandment. ..." — Matthew 22:36-40 NIV*

His first word regarding the commandment was "Love." It is the guiding tool for the application of the Law. The Jews thought the highest application of the Law was obedience. The law condemns us, but it is love that gives us life. They operated their entire culture with this in mind. It focused on the word rather the intent. So devoted were they to follow the Law, they created what was called the Torah, a fence around the Law, made up of over 600 laws to prevent a person from violating the Ten Commandments. For example, we weren't allowed to wear jewelry on the Sabbath, because if it came off we would be considered working by picking it up.

Shriveled hand healed

This complexity was putting the Law ahead of people. It seems crazy but that as how they looked at it. That's why when Jesus healed a man on the Sabbath it was such an offense. They would prefer to see the man continue with a shriveled hand or crippled legs than do any work. Ask the man with the withered hand his opinion? People can be such unreasonable souls and certainly more unfeeling. Jesus set the record straight

> *"He said to them, "If any of you has a sheep and it falls into a pit on the Sabbath, will you not take hold of it and lift it out? How lawful to do good on the Sabbath. How*

> *much more valuable is a person than a*
> *sheep! Therefore, it is lawful to do good on*
> *the Sabbath."* — Matthew 12:11-12 NIV

Jesus was all about putting people first. He reset the role of the Sabbath and implemented God's intent. God's intimate love is the defining force. He loves us and would move mountains to help us.

Putting people first

Jesus used an example that He thought they would understand. Surely we wouldn't leave sheep or lost a cow in the ditch and wait until after sundown. But that's just Jesus' way, putting people first.

It is a battle between what is subjective and what is objective. One is measurable, provable and another takes more time to think of the options. It is kind of like the difference between the game checkers and chess. In chess we must consider several moves in advance to be successful. In checkers, we can play along just responding to the moves of the other person. At first glance other than the shape of the pieces which appear different, the game board appears the same. But that is where the similarity ends. It is the strategy that sets the games apart.

Psychologists refer to the intellectual need as using the slow brain vs. the fast brain. In life we jump to conclusions as it takes minimal amounts of energy for the brain to consider it's response. Our brain uses more energy in the body than any other part and is quite miserly when it comes to access. That unfortunately means the reference to "following my gut" when making decisions the "gut" is often fatally flawed. Our first answer is probably wrong because we haven't thought through the possible consequences, we're using our fast brain which is great for routine actions because the actions are probably tried and true.

That is the problem with following the law is can be so automatic we don't take into considerations involved. We are stripped from the things which may define the reasoning behind the actions and the reasoning of future response. We are just on auto pilot. That is the problem with sentencing guidelines. To be tougher on crime because a judge is typically too lenient when it comes to sentencing we tie his hands when there is a case that requires more intervention. And can result in what appears or could be an unfair ruling. This absolute predictable type of ruling move is referred to legalism. It is not just confined to the courtroom.

Our first response is probably wrong

While the church acts as though they have a corner on the market when it comes to legalism, the truth is it is much broader in its application and goes back to ancient China to find is origins. Legalism in ancient China was a philosophical belief that human beings are more inclined to do wrong than right because they are motivated entirely by self-interest and require strict laws to control their impulses. It doesn't sound much different than the rules of a church, they just use it as a rationale to earn heaven.

Humans just need a platform of slowing down justice or judgement to consider all the facts before either legislating new policy and sentences or taking a course of action. The brain wants to pre-judge and move quicker and expedient to conserve energy it is a survival technique that keeps the warehouse full if it is needed. But tends to keep us in old habits, patterns, and familiar beliefs, and routines, like racism.

Jesus was in a constant battle with beliefs that date back for hundreds if not thousands of years. Humanity held on to the concept of earning their way to heaven because they had been fine tuning their response to the law for so long. When Jesus healed a man on the Sabbath it was considered horrible totally ignoring the human side of the event, the man could walk after years of paralysis.

That was the fast brain reacting to the protection of the law. However, love says in lieu of the man receiving his strength again we will forego the requirements of the law, after all Jesus said when he responded to the situation, said that the Sabbath is for the man, not man for the Sabbath. The Sabbath was meant as a time of rest and worship of God, not as a dictator confining or defining our lives.

In What Ways Does God Prove He Cares About Me?

_____

_____

_____

_____

_____

_____

_____

_____

_____

_____

_____

_____

_____

_____

_____

_____

_____

Being Stressed Out

"Do not conform to the pattern of this world but be transformed by the renewing of your mind." — Romans 12:2 NIV

FEAR IS KIND of tricky. We face it all the time. We never seek it, but it seeks us, troubles us, keeps us awake at night. It raises our blood pressure, gives us a headache, and can give us a sour stomach. There are so many physical manifestations for something that starts on our head. Worry can become chronic in nature, causing even long-lasting physical problems.

One agency defines fear as a feeling of emotional or physical tension. And it can come from any event or thought that makes us feel frustrated, angry, or nervous. Stress is our body's reaction to a challenge or demand. In short bursts, stress can be positive, such as when it helps us avoid danger or meet a deadline.

Stress is common

The temptation is just to get tough and determine not to worry. But that just doesn't work, we've all tried. A few years ago, I drew an analogy between many things for which we identify stress as the culprit of future problems. I saw a complex commonality between stress and what people experience as I found in buildings, bridges, and aircraft. When they find stress fractures on a bridge or aircraft, I can't help wondering if people don't have stress fractures, too. I reached out to an architect to verify my definition and he thought I had it right. I think unless we can correctly define the core of the problem our chances of mitigating a response that minimizes its impact is low.

Stress simply stated is an imbalance between load and support. Therefore, there are only two aspects of stress that we need to honestly evaluate an address. We should look at what is troubling us and either we need to reduce the load or increase the support. Sometimes we cannot reduce the load. Like St. Francis of Assis when he offered his prayer of serenity. He lived in 1200's AD but his words are part of the analysis.

> "God, grant me the grace to accept with
> serenity the things I cannot change,
> Courage to change the things I can,
> And wisdom to know the difference."

This is where an honest evaluation as St. Francis, proposes, comes into play. The first challenge in reducing our load is to consider if it is something we can affect change about it. A deadline at work may not be adjustable, but if we asked for some more time, it might be. Giving us more time or completing a related project only ensures quality work rather than quick. That reminds me of the whole adage, "we can have it quick or cheap or good, pick two." The Apostle Paul said:

> *"Do not be anxious about anything, but in every situation, by prayer and petition, with thanksgiving, present your requests to God."* — Philippians 4:6 NIV

We can't have it all. Acceptance is a powerful enough tool but cannot always be maintained over a long period. Stress becomes a monster that demands our attention if we leave and helpful for short periods of time. And Philippians is easier to say than to do. Worry and doubt is a fine art to maintain.

Polite coworkers

I used to work as what was then called a "yellow jacket" at the Mercantile Exchange in Chicago. It was where stocks were traded much like we see on the Wall Street movies. Each day I would go to the trading floor when the trading had already begun among certain stocks. My job was to run to my trader to register his purchase or sale. It wasn't glamorous, it was grunt work at best. But one thing I remember was riding up the escalator to a room full of hundreds of people shouting and how hearing their voices raised my anxiety level.

Once I got to my station and settled in, I was able to calm down. Not because the voices grew quieter or I had gotten used to the noise but because while the shouting was there all day, the traders were also among the kindest most polite people I had ever met. They may have bumped into us in a frenzy of activity, yet they were quick to say they were sorry and excuse themselves to get from the trading area to the registration area and back again.

There are times and jobs where we have periods that make us pull our hair out, but that kind of stress probably builds our character and makes us stronger. However, a heavy load that exceeds the limits may eventually make the bridge come crashing down. Whether it is a building or a bridge or a person nobody can take too heavy a load. Sometimes it is too heavy from the start or sometimes it is a load that gradually makes an impact, we decide.

We must reduce the load, take breaks, quit certain projects or slowdown to survive. If we don't cracks will begin to appear in the quality of our effort whether as a stay-at-home mom/dad or a company decision we make.

If we have children, they may suffer as we reduce time spent in their development. But as I mentioned earlier this is only half the equation. Reducing the load means by limiting responsibilities. The next step is increasing our support.

This is not granting us permission to take a greater load, but to help us with our current load. We will reduce stress by increasing support literally by the involvement of others. Stress is real but it can be broken up into less weighty parts. Each component can be separated into a division and reassigned. Jesus did not do it alone. He selected his apostles to share in the distribution of the message. But it even predates to a moment when Moses tried to do it all. His Father-in-Law gave Moses some advice:

> *"The next day Moses took his seat to serve as judge for the people, and they stood around him from morning till evening. When his father-in-law saw all that Moses was doing for the people, he said, 'What is this you are doing for the people? Why do you alone sit as judge, while all these people stand around you from morning till evening?'*
>
> *Moses answered him, 'Because the people come to me to seek God's will. Whenever*

they have a dispute, it is brought to me, and I decide between the parties and inform them of God's decrees and instructions.' Moses' father-in-law replied, 'What you are doing is not good. You and these people who come to you will only wear yourselves out. The work is too heavy for you; you cannot handle it alone.

Listen now to me and I will give you some advice, and may God be with you. You must be the people's representative before God and bring their disputes to him. Teach them his decrees and instructions and show them the way they are to live and how they are to behave. But select capable men from all the people—men who fear God, trustworthy men who hate dishonest gain—and appoint them as officials over thousands, hundreds, fifties and tens'" — Exodus 1:13-21NIV

Support

With great care Moses' Father-in-Law gently nudges Moses into sharing the load. This is a lesson for all of us. Share the load among many supporters. In bridge and building construction we will notice there are all types of support included and while they might vary as to appearance, they accomplish the same purpose. Holding it up so it can endure. Not just for now but for lifetimes. God offers all sorts of encouragement to lean on Him not just during the tough times but anytime.

Attributed to many people with various versions the saying, was found on a plaque of Former President Regan of something he heard Truman saying. The earliest version of the saying will suffice. Father Strickland, a Jesuit Priest wrote in a diary in 1863, the famous words....

> "A man may do an immense deal of good, if he does not care who gets the credit for it."

Sound familiar? It is often quoted in different ways, but we get the idea. With one ageless comment in a diary, Father Strickland set the tone for future versions and for the concept of modern-day delegation and collaboration. Not to mention the road to stress reduction. It isn't just someone to complain to but someone to help. The physical and mental assistance to accomplish the goal.

How does this play into the personal nature of God? God knows us will have trouble even now. He didn't sugar coat it.

"I have told you these things, so that in me you may have peace. In this world you will have trouble. But take heart! I have over-come the world." — John 16:33 NIV

Reduce the load

Living in this world will have its ups and downs. But He cares for us and Jesus knows we can not only face troubles but have peace at the same time. That's right when things go wrong or are not according to our plan, "Take heart."

He cares about our worries and our state of mind. He offers sweet relief just by knowing we are not alone. This was clearly demonstrated with His promise,

"...Not by might, nor by power, but by my spirit, saith the Lord of hosts." — Zechariah 4:6 KJV

When things look like there impossible to us, it's because we can only see what has been revealed to us through our experience and that of others. God oper-ates on a whole different level. If He needs something He just makes it. He is not limited to what we know to be true. He wrote the laws of physics. If he needs to bend time to comply with his plan, so be it. If He chooses to make water a solid, He can do it. He may do what He wants when He wants to. But that is according to His plan for us.

Even Jesus was faced with the sovereignty of God. There He is, with only hours remaining before He will be arrested and tortured so badly that Matthew records His words,

> *"Going a little farther, he fell with his face to the ground and prayed, "My Father, if it is possible, may this cup be taken from me. Yet not as I will, but as you will." —* Matthew 26:39 NIV

He knew the words of Isaiah that described His image so ripped open that we couldn't recognize Him. Even Jesus was subservient to the will of God. What we can control we should. What we can't, give to Jesus. This weighed heavily on Jesus, and His anxiety rose. But the Bible is clear that Jesus suffered, so that we would not have to. Whatever we feel today He had more.

> *"Peace I leave with you; my peace I give you. I do not give to you as the world gives. Do not let your hearts be troubled and do not be afraid." —* John 14:27 NIV

In What Ways Does God Prove He Cares About Me?

_____

_____

_____

_____

_____

_____

_____

_____

_____

_____

_____

_____

_____

_____

_____

_____

_____

_____

The Sovereignty of God

*"When the Advocate comes, whom I will
send to you from the Father—the Spirit of
truth who goes out from the Father—he
will testify about me."* — John 15:26 NIV

ONE OF THE most misunderstood persons of the
trinity is the Holy Spirit. Now if your unfamiliar with
the term you might be thinking of Halloween and
ghosts and haunting. But once again God was thinking
through His heart. It made His Presence unlimited to
His Followers at a time when they were most vulnerable.
Jesus was the Son of God, and He was about to
be scourged then ultimately crucified. This eve of His
death is one like a parent worry's about their children.
That is why He is laser focused on what about these
people need who gave up everything.

This promise is a demonstration of God's care. He
was concerned about their ability to survive or even

thrive. And when we consider the growth model, soon the followers would be too large and unmanageable. Jesus was limited by His physical Presence so the answer would be to send a power and comforter that could live inside them.

He is concerned about us over Himself

Picture Jesus the night of His arrest. He wants to share the Passover (Seder) with His followers. They thought He was going to share some of the traditional aspects of the meal, they thought He would share some the symbolism of the event. But He offers a greater promise.

> *"If you love me, keep my commands. And I will ask the Father, and he will give you another advocate to help you and be with you forever, the Spirit of truth. The world cannot accept him because it neither sees him nor knows him. But you know him, for he lives with you and will be in you. I will not leave you as orphans; I will come to you."* — John 14:15-18 NIV

I'd like to point out the love that God exudes in this twelfth hour. His concern was they would not be left as "orphans." In so doing He promises an internal indwelling of the Holy Spirit. This a message of love much like what Jesus said from the cross, when during His own agony, His concern is about the thieves on the cross and their spiritual life. He even asks John to adopt the wellbeing of His mother. It was the heartbeat of God to care for others.

So now we translate that into our lives today. He cares so much about us, way more then He cares for Himself. He not only wants us to surrender to Him but allow the Holy Spirit to live inside of us. But can the Holy Spirit provide to help us?

> *"But the Advocate, the Holy Spirit, whom the Father will send in my name, will teach you all things and will remind you of everything I have said to you." — John14:26*

God is not limited

One of the most obvious benefits of the Holy Spirit is God is no longer limited by the geographic constraints. He can move among His people by His Presence. This is even better then when He walked in Eden. People today are separated by thousands of miles, only a plane flight away for sure but if we must walk to be there that isn't enough. Ask any parent, in a crisis we can't get there fast enough.

One Wild night

One day my young family and I were coming home from a midweek church service. You can imagine all the energy that just blew into my house by four elementary aged children. My oldest opened the door of the refrigerator too fast. A jar in the door comes flying off the shelf and impacts the floor, shattering once it hits the floor. What's worse is that a shard of glass lacerated Lori's foot. It bled so much immediately we knew she would need stitches.

So, I swept her up in my arms and headed for the door. I offered her comfort as we went while my wife grabbed the car keys. We worked like clockwork. Calm and focused, that is until we got to the emergency department. There we sat and waited with a towel wrapped around Lori's foot. I was so proud of the speed in which we acted. Then in the quietness of the moment it was like that scene in Home Alone, when the mom shouts "Kevin!" because she realizes he was left behind accidentally. We had left three kids behind at home alone and in the rush their last glimpse of their sister being hurriedly ushered out the door. We called our neighbors, and they came over to our home, so it was covered, thankfully.

That night our parenting instincts blinded us to anything else. God feels the same about us. Everything else is secondary to our wellbeing in God's eyes.

> *"Because you are his sons, God sent the*
> *Spirit of his Son into our hearts, the*
> *Spirit who calls out, "Abba, Father." —*
> *Galatians 4:6 NIV*

He doesn't refer to us as second-rate or first-rate citizens. Rather He uses personal pronouns to describe our relationship. Then He tells us to call Him papa or daddy, not Father. There is nothing wrong with the word, "father," but when we want our child to feel like they can come to us with warmth, we skip the formality and would use an informal address. As in this case God is giving us permission to bring down the curtain that divides, not disrespectfully, but out of affection.

God's love is incredible. He wants us to know his presence is with us always, but in what ways? He can only be in one place at a time. That's what we think. Jesus told us that be because if He goes away, He can send another. The Holy Spirit can be in us and all around us.

Living inside and leading us

The Holy Spirit was intended to support us in several ways. First of all, there is the role of teacher.

> *"But the Advocate, the Holy Spirit, whom*
> *the Father will send in my name, will*
> *teach you all things and will remind*

you of everything I have said to you." —
John 14:26. NIV

We are always growing. Learning what to do and
how to interact with Life's big questions. The Holy
Spirit always tells us what to do and say in each situation. He teaches and gives us the words to use as we
face challenges. Even though we may doubt ourself, He
promised to give Moses his brother, Aaron, as a helper
with what to say and with his strength he led one million people out of slavery. He gave words to Isaiah even
though he had never spoken up before and became one
the most celebrated prophets of the Old Testament.

But this is kind of like a twofer. Because not only
does He tell us what to say or the source of our peace,
He speaks for us as our advocate. Our name this day is
spoken in heaven:

> *"Nevertheless, I tell you the truth; It is expe-*
> *dient for you that I go away: for if I go not*
> *away, the Comforter will not come unto*
> *you; but if I depart, I will send him unto*
> *you." — John 16:7 NIV*

Secondly, Jesus offered one more assurance, He not
only promised the Holy Spirit, God wants us to know
we will find the comforter. Holy Spirit power is great,
the teaching can be welcome, and the advocacy will

be important, but the role as comforter is so practical for us in our daily routine. We could really use some assurances.

Another assurance that He is a personal God. He calls us to help others provides us with resources to accomplish His calling, words with which people will either accept the plan God has or deny Him. So, every part fits and has a purpose, kind of like the Disney movie that talks about the circle of life.

Circle of life

The Circle of Life, is a philosophical concept, and means that we start at the end and end in the beginning. Our lives, from beginning to end resemble a complete full circle. No matter how big or small the circle is, it ends in the exact same way for everyone.

Simply put every event has a purpose. We might not see how it fits, but like pieces of a puzzle if we could step back far enough, we can see the bigger picture. Sometimes it isn't even in our lifetime, but somewhere along the line we will eventually be able to say," Oh yeah, that's why."

A simple physical example of the circle is found in the cycle of life and is something we learned in grade school. Forests reduce soil erosion and are watered by the rain which comes from the oceans and are heated up then reach the cold air and fall from the sky as raindrops to run off back into the oceans and the cycle starts again. Forests are one among an almost limitless number of examples of the web or circle of life on our planet.

Can we imagine how complicated it must be for God to manage the world without violating man's free-will? It is a long game. Man keeps on changing the rules making the correlations even more difficult. He even makes decisions that are in complete opposition to God's plan. God tries to keep us on track than man moves the goal posts.

No wonder it has taken thousands of years to order our steps. Each of us who surrender to Jesus have a role to play, Paul talked about it like this,

> "Now if the foot should say, "Because I am not a hand, I do not belong to the body," it would not for that reason stop being part of the body. And if the ear should say, "Because I am not an eye, I do not belong to the body," it would not for that reason stop being part of the body. If the whole body were an eye, where would the sense of hearing be? If the whole body were an ear, where would the sense of smell be? But in fact, God has placed the parts in the body, every one of them, just as he wanted them to be. If they were all one part, where would the body

be? As it is, there are many parts, but one body." — Corinthians 12:15-20

We see the Bible says we have value right where we are. This isn't just words of comfort. It is our marching orders that instead of complaining, we should be looking at our current situation and consider God might need us right where we are. Jail cell, hospital bed, living room, or elsewhere. If God desires to touch everyone in the world, wouldn't it just make sense, he needs spokes-people everywhere? People who love Him and want to serve Him.

I know it is only natural to want to improve oneself. But we are talking about something bigger than ourselves. Something that is supernatural. Something larger than our decisions or visions of greatness. We will only find peace if we line ourselves with God's plan and stop fighting it for what the world offers us.

This is hard for me to write when I am still recovering from a stroke only six months ago. But let me put that into perspective. I am taking the time to write my thoughts and God's wishes for us. Every therapist is an opportunity to share the good news in case they have not heard. I can inspire people with my limited mobility and positive spirit, even if they are a Christ follower. I am taking the saying, "bloom where we're planted," literally.

I have a choice to bemoan these events of what are on the surface hard, the limited left side strength, halted steps, no job, etc. Or evaluate what I can do, like the song, The Little Drummer Boy," and take what I have and offer them to His service.

Wet ground faith

While God promises to give us what we need when we need it may require a bit of faith on our part. There are abundant examples in the Word of God but let me give us one. We've have probably heard of in a story, The parting of the Red Sea on command was big. Israel was on the move and the Pharoah of Egypt changed his mind and wanted the slaves back. So out go the chariots closing in on anywhere between 600,000 and one million people with their backs up against the waters. When the waters parted, and Israel walked across on dry land.

The Bible says when the feet of the people touched the water then the waters parted. They had to step into a non-parted sea before it parted. Did God supply the need? Of course, He did, but the people had to act first.

If I am just patient, sometimes I want to cram the word patience right down their throat, things will be for the best. Can we relate to both thoughts? Are we in a spot we would rather not be and wonder if God knows or cares? Do we even feel we deserve the situation? Like every good news/bad news joke we are reminded of this world situation. When will it end?

> *"I have told you these things, so that in me you may have peace. In this world you will have trouble. But take heart! I have over-come the world."* — John 16:33 NIV

The Bad news first, Jesus gave us a heads up by saying, "In this world you will have trouble…" There is no doubt in case we thought Amazon would solve all our problems. There is no doubt that we will face adversity. Things will go wrong, count on it. How we respond is the question. With all the assurance He can muster He says, but wait, "But take heart, I have over-come the world." There will be a silver lining, it just may take some time.

I have bad days too

We have good days of optimism and have depressed days of doubt. Our life is a journey, full of uphill bat-tles and downhill racing. But in all this God is still on the throne. Today my job search is one of applications, but only for jobs where I can help people. For much of my life I have followed the money. Now I want to matter, demonstrate purpose, and make my job search rule to follow, love. Can I say my adversity has made me a better person? Absolutely! But I am still working on the patience part.

In What Ways Does God Prove He Cares About Me?

_____

_____

_____

_____

_____

_____

_____

_____

_____

_____

_____

_____

_____

_____

_____

_____

_____

_____

We Are Not Alone

I can't think of a better way to end a book than to say:

Jesus loves us.
When all hope is gone

Jesus loves us
When we don't know the next steps

Jesus loves us
If we are facing the worst tragedy ever

Jesus loves us